COOKBOOK FOR KIDS

COOKBOOK FOR KIDS

Hilary Brown
and
the Editors of Consumer Reports Books

Consumers Union, Mount Vernon, New York

For
Nicola and Andrew Brown
and
Daniel and Scott Leonard

Cookbook for Kids is a Consumer Reports Book published by Consumers Union, the nonprofit organization that publishes *Consumer Reports,* the monthly magazine of test reports, product Ratings, and buying guidance. Established in 1936, Consumers Union is chartered under the Not-For-Profit Corporation Law of the State of New York.

The purposes of Consumers Union, as stated in its charter, are to provide consumers with information and counsel on consumer goods and services, to give information on all matters relating to the expenditure of the family income, and to initiate and to cooperate with individual and group efforts seeking to create and maintain decent living standards.

Consumers Union derives its income solely from the sale of *Consumer Reports* and other publications. In addition, expenses of occasional public service efforts may be met, in part, by nonrestrictive, noncommercial contributions, grants, and fees. Consumers Union accepts no advertising or product samples and is not beholden in any way to any commercial interest. Its Ratings and reports are solely for the use of the readers of its publications. Neither the Ratings nor the reports nor any Consumers Union publications, including this book, may be used in advertising or for any commercial purpose. Consumers Union will take all steps open to it to prevent such uses of its material, its name, or the name of *Consumer Reports.*

Contents

Introduction for Adults

Learning how to follow printed instructions is a major requirement of education. When learning how to follow a printed recipe—which is, after all, a set of instructions—more than cooking is learned. Sensory, conceptual, and motor skills are exercised, and imagination and creative thinking are stimulated. All of these help to make cooking a very satisfying and rewarding activity.

Our experience tells us that many children would like to learn how to cook. Would like to learn, that is, if they can have a little fun doing it; if they can follow the instructions with ease; and if it's not going to take too much time. And—this is important—there is an element of surprise involved. In *Cookbook for Kids* there are plenty of surprises: corn muffins made with canned corn; hamburger cooked with grape jelly; cake frosting made from candy bars. Not your usual sponge cake, brownies, or plain fudge here. The recipes in this book are planned to be unusual enough to attract the interest of children 8 through 13 and to cover a variety of tastes and needs.

Also—and perhaps best of all—these recipes just might send some young cooks on a lifetime adventure in the kitchen.

How the recipes were tested

The forty recipes in *Cookbook for Kids* were tested by the children of Consumers Union's staff and by 65 subscribers to CU's publication for young consumers, *Penny Power*.

Each tester was supplied with one recipe, and a questionnaire to be completed and returned to us after the recipe had been prepared. The questionnaire was comprised of several "yes or no" questions such as: Have you ever cooked from a recipe before? Did you need help from an adult while preparing the recipe? Were the directions easy to follow? Did you like preparing the recipe? Did you have any problems? Did you like the taste of what you prepared? (The replies to this last question ranged from "I loved it" to "I hated it.")

Every questionnaire returned to us was seriously considered. The amount of information conveyed by the questionnaires (from girls and boys all over the

United States) was truly staggering. They told us—often in *very* direct language —how to improve the recipe; what ingredient was used in place of the ingredient called for; how certain steps in the directions could be combined; and, perhaps most important, why they enjoyed preparing the recipe.

Introduction for Children

This cookbook is exciting and fun because it has new and different recipes in it. And cooking can be exciting and it can be fun.

You don't need to know how to cook to use this book. If you have used a recipe before you will be familiar with some of the traps a recipe can set. For example, if the directions in a recipe say "beat the egg whites and fold them into the meringue"—how long do you beat the egg whites? How do you "fold"? And, what exactly is meringue? *Cookbook for Kids* presents the recipes with NO traps. If the directions in a recipe say "fold," we show you how with pictures and words. If the directions say "beat the egg whites," you know how long to beat them because the recipe will tell you what they should be like after beating: "Beat until the egg whites are stiff enough to stand up in points."

Equipment and many ingredients are illustrated so you can match as closely as possible what is available in your kitchen to what is called for in the recipe. Most recipes give "substitute" ingredients in case you don't have—or can't find—the ingredients listed in the recipe.

This is what shows you how easy, moderately easy, or not-so-easy a recipe is:

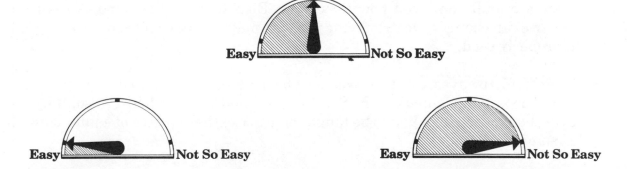

No ages are used because if you're 9 years old and have helped out a lot in the kitchen, you probably can follow a recipe better than somebody 13 years old who has never boiled water and who is found in the kitchen only when it's time to eat.

Safety tips

- Always read the entire recipe from beginning to end. This way, you can check if you have all the necessary equipment, ingredients, and time. It also shows you in advance any trouble spots where you might need help or supervision from an adult.

- Always keep measuring cups on a flat surface when pouring in an ingredient. Never hold the measuring cups (or spoons) over the bowl or pot that holds your other measured ingredients.

- If you have little or no experience chopping food with sharp knives, have an adult show you how. Once you get used to the care needed, you will become more comfortable about the chore. In fact, many cooks find that chopping, and dicing, and shredding can be fun. Of course, you can always use a pair of kitchen scissors (all the best chefs have a pair).

- If your experience with electric kitchen gadgets is limited, it's a good idea to have an adult show you how they work. Blenders, electric hand beaters, electric can openers, electric frying pans are magical time and energy savers if properly used.

- Ovens, microwaves, toasters, and most heating equipment used in kitchens often need adult supervision. So, speak up and ask for help. Absolutely everybody who cooks had to be taught how to use these pieces of equipment at some time.

- Remember—anything that is "turned on" must be "turned off."

- Keep all pot handles turned toward the back of the stove and turned away from the edges of countertops or tabletops. This avoids messy—and perhaps painful—accidents.

- Always have plenty of potholders or oven gloves available and within easy reach.

Being creative in the kitchen is an experience everyone should practice at least a little. So go ahead—be creative, have some fun, and fix yourself something to eat.

Cooking Terms

Creaming: to beat or whip fat and sugar together so that they have the consistency of fluffy cream. When enough air has been mixed in, the mixture reaches the correct very pale color of cream.

Cube: to cut into small squares (approximately ½ to 1 inch in size).

Dice: to cut into pieces smaller than ½-inch cubes.

Dot or dab: drop bits of butter, or cheese and the like, here and there over food (see page 84).

Fold: to blend 2 ingredients in 1 bowl into a single mixture by *gently* lifting them up and over again and again in a circular motion, with a large spoon or a single beater. This is *not* stirring or beating or whipping (see page 101).

Knead: to work and press a mass of dough with the hands. Place the dough on a lightly-floured surface and mold it into a fairly flat ball. Place the heel of your hand in the center of the ball and push as hard as you can *away* from you. Then fold it to make a new ball. Turn the ball slightly to your left or right and continue pushing. Turn the dough over occasionally.

Oven temperatures: Very low, 200 to 250°F. Low, 275 to 325°F. Moderate, 350 to 400°F (most baking). Hot, 425 to 475°F (puff pastries). Very hot, 500°F and up (broiling).

Puree: to reduce a solid ingredient to a thin paste in a blender (apples to applesauce, for instance).

Sauté: to cook in a low-sided pan, like a frying pan, in a small amount of any fat.

Separate: to separate the yolk of an egg from the white using the egg shells or a cup.

Shred: to cut or tear into strips.

Sift: to put an ingredient (usually flour) into a sifter (a sieve) and scatter evenly into a bowl or over another ingredient.

Toss: to mix over and over—usually applies only to salads. (It does *not* mean to throw—as one tosses a ball.)

COOKBOOK FOR KIDS

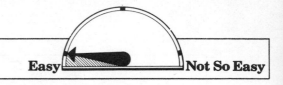
Belle's No-Bake Chocolate Cookies

This is the only recipe in this book that was not created especially for this book. It came from a friend called Belle Lieberman. Thank you, Mrs. Lieberman.

Servings: 3 dozen cookies.

Equipment

2-quart pot

bowl (about 4-quart size)

wax paper

1-tablespoon measure

1-teaspoon measure

4-cup measure

wooden spoon

Ingredients

2 cups sugar

½ cup milk

1 stick butter

pinch of salt

2 teaspoons vanilla extract

3 cups quick oats

1 cup chopped nuts (4-ounce can)

1 can coconut flakes (6- or 8-ounce can)

3 tablespoons cocoa powder

2

Directions

1. Put sugar, milk, butter, salt, and vanilla in the pot.

2. Bring to a boil over a high heat, stirring all the time to make sure the bottom does not burn.

3. After it has come to a boil, take it off the heat, and put to one side. Turn off the heat.

4. Measure the 3 cups of oats into the bowl.

5. Add the nuts and the coconut flakes.

6. Add into this mixture the 3 tablespoons of cocoa powder. Stir well.

7. Pour the cooked mixture over the oat mixture in the bowl and stir well until everything is blended. It will look and feel fairly sticky.

8. Place a long piece of wax paper on the countertop.

9. Using a regular teaspoon, drop spoonfuls of the mixture onto the wax paper. Leave some space for the mixture to spread out a bit.

10. Cool before you eat. These cookies can be stored in a tin with a tight lid with a piece of wax paper between the layers.

3

Substitutes

Milk

You can use skim milk—the results are the same.

Butter

You can use margarine—the texture is the same, but the cookies will taste different. The taste change will depend on the margarine you use. *Imperial* margarine gives results nearest to butter.

Salt

You can leave this out—most people won't know the difference.

Oats, coconut, nuts

You can substitute different cereals and different nuts. You can omit the coconut.

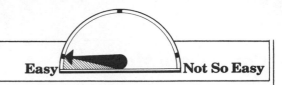

Easy — Not So Easy

Corny Corn Muffins

Here's a recipe that uses canned creamed corn to make tasty corn muffins.

Servings: 12 muffins.

Equipment

paper towel

1 12-cup muffin pan

teaspoon

1-cup measure

large mixing bowl

sifter

whisk

Ingredients

2 tablespoons oil

approximately 6 teaspoons flour

1 cup Bisquick

1 egg

1 8-ounce can creamed corn

¼ cup milk

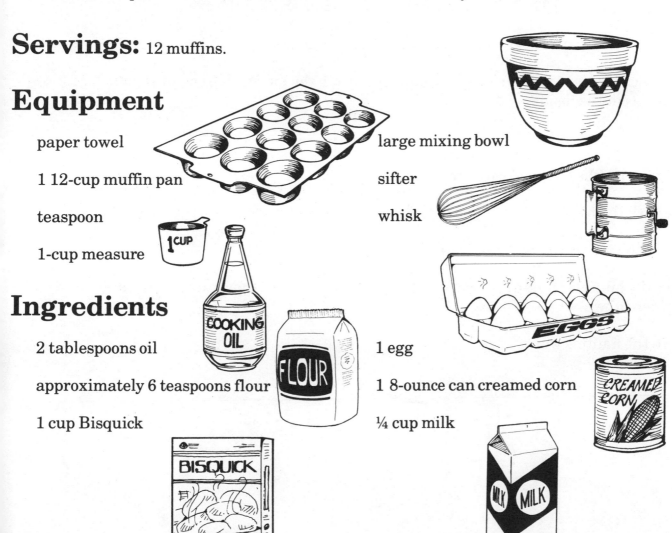

5

Directions

1. Preheat the oven to 375°F. Make sure there is a middle shelf in the oven.

2. With a piece of paper towel, oil the insides of the muffin cups.

3. Put about ½ teaspoon flour into each cup. Gently tap the muffin cups against your hand to coat the inside.

4. Put the Bisquick into the bowl and stir with the whisk to break up any lumps.

5. Add the egg, the creamed corn, and the milk.

6. Mix with the whisk.

7. Divide the mixture equally into all the muffin cups.

8. Place the muffins in the oven and bake for 20 minutes or until they are risen and are a golden brown.

9. Serve the muffins warm.

Substitutes

Muffins

These muffins can be made into pancakes simply by dropping the batter by the spoonful onto a hot greased griddle. Use a large spoon. When the edges of the pancakes start getting that cooked, dry look, turn them over with a spatula. Great with syrup poured over them.

Helpful Hints

There is one important thing you should keep in mind when using canned creamed corn in a recipe for a baked goodie. You can never tell *exactly* how much corn, and how much liquid, you are going to get. So when adding the milk to this recipe for muffins, do not add it all at once. There isn't much milk anyway, but start to stir the flour, corn, and *some* of the milk until you are sure the batter is too thick, then add the rest of the milk and stir well. On the other hand, you may get a can of corn with more corn than liquid, then you may need a bit *more* milk than the recipe calls for.

The idea is to get a batter that is a bit like a *very thick* New England clam chowder: It may look thick, but when you lift it by the spoonful, it is runnier than it looks.

And remember not to overmix. Just enough so all the dry ingredients are wet. You may have an odd lump or so, but not to worry—they'll disappear in the baking. So, don't overmix.

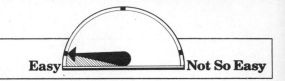

Easy ◄────── Not So Easy

Frozen Fruits and Marshmallow Fluff

Here's a snack for fruit lovers (or for those of you who don't like fruit much but are willing to try something new). And *anyone* who crunches the ice in a drink will like these frozen fruit snacks. And for those who can't live without marshmallows just wait until you try *frozen* marshmallow fluff.

Servings: any number.

Equipment

1 or 2 shallow trays (similar to cookie sheets)

foil paper

teaspoon

can opener

Ingredients

1 banana

1 bunch seedless grapes

1 small can of pineapple rings

1 small can of peach halves

juice from ½ lemon (fresh or reconstituted)

1 jar of marshmallow fluff

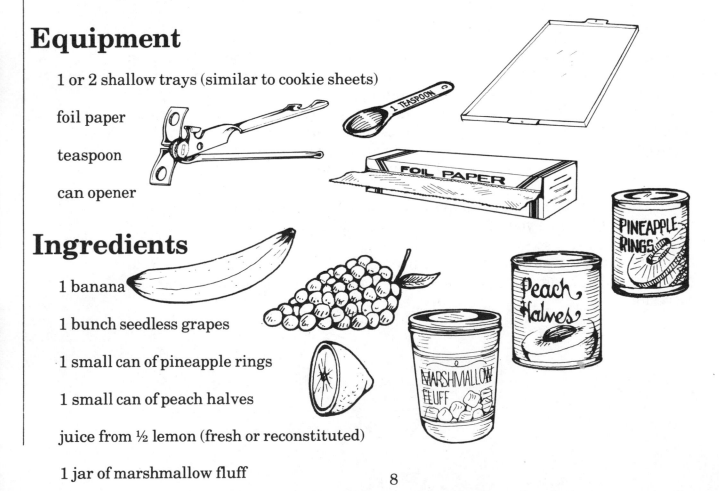

8

Directions

1. Make sure there is a space in the freezer for one or two trays.

2. Check the grapes to remove old ones, and the stalks if you like, but that's not necessary.

3. Place the grapes uncovered on one of the trays.

4. Peel the banana.

5. Sprinkle it with lemon juice, and smooth the juice over the banana with your fingers.

6. Wrap it smoothly in foil, and put it also on the tray.

7. Open the can of peaches and the can of pineapple.

8. Drain the juices into a glass. (You can drink the juice later if you want.)

9. Wrap each piece of fruit carefully without wrinkling the foil and place on the tray.

10. Spoon as much marshmallow fluff—in teaspoon-size dabs—as you want on a sheet of foil. Cover with another sheet of foil, and place on the same tray if there's room. If not, use another tray.

11. All of this goes into the freezer.

12. The fruit takes at least four hours to freeze. The fluff takes longer than four hours to freeze and never really gets hard. (If you are going to eat the fruit within two days you do not need to wrap it at all—it dries rapidly in the freezer and forms a surface coat.)

If you prepare the fruit or the fluff at night, you can have a snack the next day.

Substitutes

Fruit

Some vegetables work as well as fruits, and so do some soft candies such as nougat. Canned litchi nuts work really well. Fresh fruits work also, but you have to sprinkle them with lemon juice. Mangoes are good, but some people find the strings or fibers in them to be a nuisance.

Helpful Hints

You could line up rows of pineapple chunks, spear them with toothpicks, and freeze them for party treats, or float them in drinks such as ginger ale or 7-UP.

You can cut a melon carefully so you have several thick slices (any kind of melon except watermelon, it has too many seeds). Use a small cookie cutter, and cut shapes out of the melon slices to freeze for treats, or to float in sodas, or for special party sherbet punch.

Other snacks that are fun to make are ice cream fruit sandwiches. Melon is the best for this because you need squares made from thick slices. Freeze them. Cut a square from a block of ice cream. Sandwich the ice cream between the melon slices.

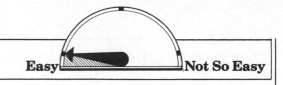
Hot Dog Biscuits

These are very quick to make, and if you take care they will look so professional that they can be served at parties. They are best hot, but can be eaten cold. And you can heat them up in a toaster oven (the kind that takes foods like whole muffins or bagels).

Servings: 8 to 10 biscuits.

Equipment

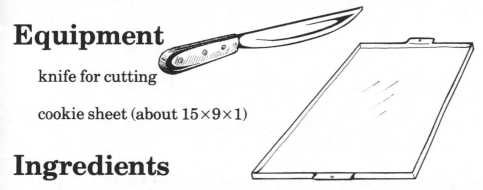

knife for cutting

cookie sheet (about 15×9×1)

Ingredients

1 container of ready-to-bake biscuits (contains 8 or 10 biscuits)

about 1 tablespoon flour

2 hot dogs

Directions

1. Preheat the oven to 400°F. Be sure there is a middle shelf in the oven.

2. Open the container of biscuits carefully. (It can make a loud noise, like a firecracker, and the little biscuits can pop out and hit you in the face.)

3. Coat your hands with a little flour to keep the biscuits from sticking to them. Spread the biscuits out on the countertop.

4. Using the heel of your hand, press each biscuit down until it is flatter and larger.

5. Cut each hot dog into 4 (or 5) pieces. You now have 8 (or 10) little pieces of hot dog.

6. Put one piece of hot dog on each biscuit. Fold the biscuit over the hot dog and pinch the edges together. You now have a biscuit that looks like a half circle.

7. Put all the biscuits on the cookie sheet, arranging them fairly close together but not too near the edge of the sheet or they might burn.

8. Put in the oven and bake for 15 to 20 minutes. They should be a golden-brown color and firm when you tap them. Turn off the oven.

Substitutes

Dough
Any kind of quick biscuit dough will do for this recipe.

Hot dogs
You can use pieces of cheese. How much cheese depends on your taste. American cheese slices work well. Cut them into small squares and stack them. A small piece of apple with a bit of cheese gives a crunchy cheese biscuit. Jams and preserves of any

kind (except those with a lot of runny juice) can be delicious in this recipe. You can also use banana, but the result is somewhat gooey.

Helpful Hints

If you think the biscuits are too large, then cut them in half. This will make twice as many hot dog biscuits.

You can always add more filling. Or flatten the dough out more and really pile the filling in. (This can be messy with jams, though.)

If you find the dough gets very sticky while you work with it, use a tablespoon of flour to coat your hands so the dough does not stick to them.

If you find it difficult to get the dough really flat, try using a rolling pin you've coated lightly with flour.

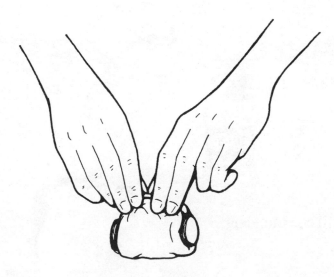

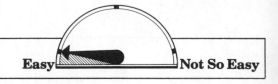
Lemonade Slush

Slushes (in case you've been living on the Moon and don't know) are drinks made of crushed ice flavored with whatever you like. You need a blender to make them, so if you have not used one before, ask someone to explain to you how to use and take care of it.

Servings: 1.

Equipment

blender

1-cup measure

wooden spoon or spatula

tall glass

scoop or tablespoon

Ingredients

powdered lemonade mix

about ½ cup of hot water

about 2 cups ice (to half fill the blender)

Directions

1. Make sure the blender is plugged in and that the top can be securely covered. (Some tops come in pieces, so check to make sure the pieces of the top are all there.)

2. Put the blender setting on "chop" or "ice."

3. Measure out 2 scoops (4 tablespoons if there's no scoop) of the lemonade mix into the measuring cup.

4. Add the hot water and stir until the mix is melted.

5. Fill the blender with ice up to the half-way mark.

6. Add the hot lemonade mix.

7. Put the top securely on the blender.

8. Push the start button.

9. It takes about 2 minutes for the blender to turn this mixture into a crushed lemon ice slush. Be very careful that the machine is off and the blades are not turning, if you have to push the ice down from the sides of the blender. Use a wooden spoon or a spatula to push the ice down from the sides of the blender and off the blades.

10. Pour into a tall glass, and sip slowly.

Substitutes

Ice

There is no substitute for ice, but you can use sherbet. If you do, add bits of fruit for flavoring, say, banana with lemon sherbet. Or try chocolate syrup with orange sherbet.

Flavoring

Any kind of fruit-flavored powder mix will do. So will fresh fruit if it's juicy.

Canned fruit can be good, but the flavor may be too mild. If you love canned pears, use them and spark the slush with grenadine syrup if there's a bottle of it in the kitchen. This makes a lovely flavor, and gives the slush a pink swirl if you add the syrup at the end by stirring it in with a spoon.

Nutrition Note

This is a marvelous recipe for giving you the fruits you should have every day.

Grenadine syrup has natural color in it. One of the reasons for adding colors to food is to make the food appetizing to look at. We often "eat with our eyes." Natural colors come mainly from other foods: red from beets, orange from carrots, and the like. Natural food colors are considered to be mostly safe—after all, people have been eating beets and carrots for years.

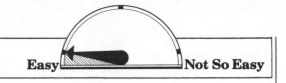
Popovers

In England these delightful puffy batters are known as Yorkshire pudding. Years and years ago they were served before the Sunday roast beef to fill everybody up so they did not need huge helpings of meat. Way back then meat was very, very expensive (it costs less now). But we still don't need as much meat as some of us think we do, so maybe popovers should make a comeback to help our health. For a hungry person in need of a quick, hot snack, these are just right.

Servings: 12 popovers.

Equipment

12-cup muffin pan

2-quart bowl

whisk

1-cup measure

Ingredients

2 or 3 tablespoons oil (enough oil to barely cover the bottom of the muffin cups)

1 cup flour

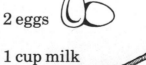

2 eggs

1 cup milk

17

Directions

1. Put a little bit of oil in each muffin cup.

2. Preheat oven to 450°F. Be sure there is a middle shelf in the oven.

3. Put the muffin pan in the oven.

4. Put all the ingredients in the bowl.

5. Whisk to mix thoroughly. By the time you have beaten the batter enough to distribute the eggs it should be smooth. (It is a fairly runny batter, like thick cream.)

6. Take the hot muffin pan out of the oven, using an oven glove or pot holder.

7. Use the 1-cup measure to ladle the batter equally into the muffin cups. The batter half-fills each cup.

8. Put the muffin pan back in the oven and bake for 20 minutes. DON'T PEEK. After 20 minutes the batter should have risen above the cup into a firm shape. The popovers will be a golden-brown and have a hole in the middle. Turn the oven off.

9. Eat as is, or drop some jam in the hole for a treat.

Substitutes

Batter

There are really no good substitutes for the batter that will give a good result. Brown or whole wheat flour doesn't puff up much. You have to find a special wheat popover recipe. What you can do is put all the batter in a regular baking pan. Add little sausages, or small meatballs. The batter does not puff up as high and can get soggy if not eaten right away. This treat is known to children in the British Isles as "Toad in the Hole."

Nutrition Note

Some people might think of this recipe for popovers as "junk food." First, there really is no such thing: If it's junk, it's not food. If it's food, it's not junk. How about sodas? How about store-bought cookies full of nothing? How about candy?

It is not the food that's junk—it's the eaters. Junky eating habits cause trouble. You need milk, and meat or fish, or poultry or eggs, lots of fresh fruits and vegetables, and breads and cereals. If you eat these, then you can safely have an occasional piece of candy or an ice cream soda, or a couple of your own popovers with jam.

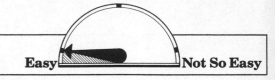
Quick Garlic Bread

This bread is good not only for a snack but as a potato substitute. It takes very little time (as long as you have a toaster), and there is no limit to the alternatives you can cook up with this recipe.

Servings: As much as you want.

Equipment

butter knife

toaster

Ingredients

2 slices white bread

2 pats butter

garlic powder

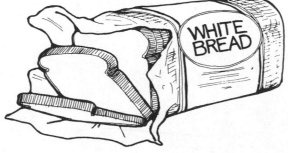

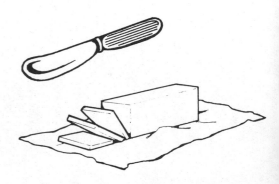

Directions

1. Spread each slice of bread with the butter. Use the amount you like, but not too thick — the bread cannot absorb too much.

2. Sprinkle garlic powder on each slice. Again, as much as you like.

3. Put the 2 slices together, put them on the counter and squash them flat. (Even if you have a toaster that can take 2 slices in one slot, you still have to squash the bread to get the slices to stick together.)

4. Use your hand to squash the bread, and move the slice around so all the crusts are squashed flat too. Soon, the bread should be thin enough to fit in the slot of the toaster.

5. Go ahead and toast it. You'll like it.

Substitutes

Bread
You can use any bread you like. (Raisin bread, however, is not recommended with garlic.)

Garlic powder
Butter goes well with a little sugar, and a little spice, like cinnamon, in place of the garlic powder. Don't use too much sugar. No more than a teaspoonful because sugar burns. And too much sugar makes a lot of black smoke. No fair for the person who has to clean up the kitchen. So be careful. Jelly or jam, for instance, can act much the same as sugar. A thin spread of cream cheese can be delicious toasted like this.

Helpful Hints

If you have a toaster oven, you can make a lot of quick tasty snacks if you think of them as open toasted sandwiches. You can pile nearly anything on a piece of bread and toast it in a toaster oven. The rule is, put the food that needs the least toasting on the bread first, then the food that needs the most toasting on top of that. This way you can pile four or five foods on the bread.

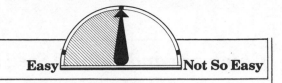
Chick-Pea and Sesame Seed Dip

This is a mixture of both, but it has very little taste of chick-peas, and very little taste of sesame seeds. Together they make a whole new taste sensation. For people who are interested in food, to discover a new food like this can be exciting.

Servings: 4 portions as an hors d'oeuvre, 8 to 10 as a dip.

Equipment

½-cup measure

knife for chopping

chopping board

blender

whisk or fork

medium-size bowl

23

Chick-pea and Sesame Seed Dip

Ingredients

1 16-ounce can of chick-peas

½ cup lemon juice (fresh or reconstituted)

2 garlic cloves, chopped

1 can sesame seed paste

Directions

1. Drain the can of chick-peas and discard the juice.

2. Put the lemon juice, the chick-peas, and the garlic into the blender. Set at "puree."

3. Add the sesame seed paste to the chick-pea and garlic mixture in the blender and puree. If the sesame paste is too thick, you may need to stir it into the mixture with a whisk or fork.

4. Put the dip in the bowl, and let it "set" for about 20 minutes. This thickens the dip a little, which makes it better, but you can eat it right away if you like.

Substitutes

Chick-peas
You could always prepare your own, boiling them from a package of dried chick-peas. But it takes about an hour to get them really soft, and then they are still hot. It's not worth it for a dip. However, dried chick-peas seem to always taste better than those from a can, so if you have the time to cook them in advance, say for a party, then try it.

Sesame paste
This is usually found in the gourmet section of supermarkets. Health food stores may have it also. If you are able to get sesame seeds, blend them with a little oil.

Helpful Hints

This is a lovely dip you can put on just about anything: bread, chips, pretzels, even fingers. But the very best thing to eat this dip with is pita bread. The next best are slices from long loaves of French or Italian bread.

The dip can keep for several days in the refrigerator. Put the whole dish in a large plastic bag and close it with a twist tie.

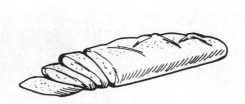

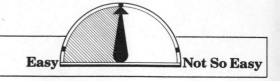
The One Egg, One Bowl Quick Cake

Cakes are basically made from flour, eggs, a liquid, sugar, and often fat such as butter, margarine, or oil. Anything else is flavoring. This cake is fun to make and simple. It is also a quick way to make a convenient fresh-baked goodie.

Servings: 1 layer cake.

Equipment

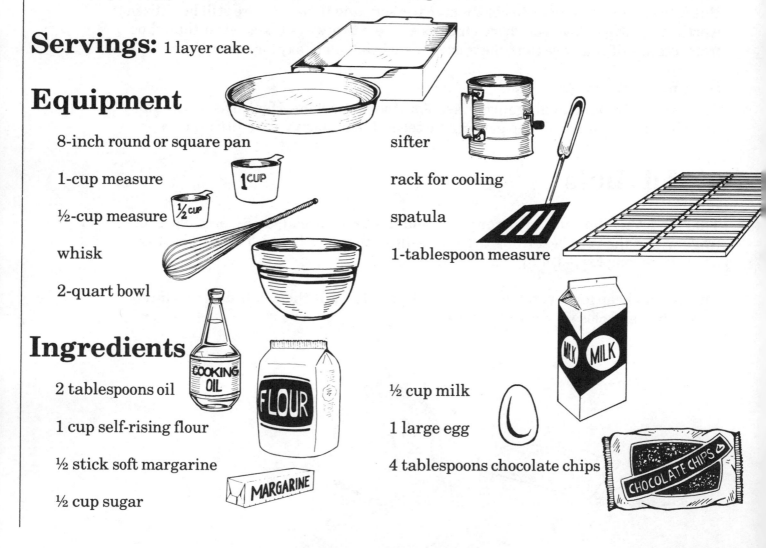

8-inch round or square pan

1-cup measure

½-cup measure

whisk

2-quart bowl

sifter

rack for cooling

spatula

1-tablespoon measure

Ingredients

2 tablespoons oil

1 cup self-rising flour

½ stick soft margarine

½ cup sugar

½ cup milk

1 large egg

4 tablespoons chocolate chips

Directions

1. Preheat the oven to 375°F. Be sure there is a middle shelf in the oven.

2. Oil the cake pan and shake a little flour into the pan to coat it lightly.

3. Sift the cup of self-rising flour into the bowl.

4. Make a well in the center of the flour.

5. Put the margarine, sugar, milk, and egg in the well.

6. Stir gently with the whisk until everything is mixed.

7. Then beat the mixture with the whisk until it is smooth. This takes about 24 strokes of the whisk around the bowl.

8. Stir in the chocolate chips with the whisk.

9. With the spatula, scrape all the mixture into the pan and spread it around evenly.

10. Make a shallow hollow in the middle of the mixture—this is to stop a peak from rising. Peaks are a nuisance when the time comes to spread the frosting.

11. Put your cake in the center of the oven.

12. Bake the cake for about 25 minutes. Turn the oven off and take the cake from the oven.

13. Cool the cake on a rack for about 15 minutes.

Continued

14. Take the cake out of the pan and let it cool completely.

15. You can frost the cake if you want to after it has cooled completely. Of course, if you're starving for cake, you can cut a piece the minute it comes from the oven. But be careful—hot chocolate chips can burn your tongue.

Substitutes

Flour

Don't use whole wheat flour for this recipe. It makes a doughy unpleasant cake. If you want a whole wheat taste, substitute 4 tablespoons of wheat germ in place of chocolate chips. (You *can* add both, but be warned: chocolate wheat germ is a taste you'll have to get used to.)

Also, you can use regular flour, but add 1¼ teaspoons of baking powder to the recipe (sift it along with the flour).

Margarine

You can use butter, but it must be left to soften at room temperature (about half an hour or more). If not, you will have trouble whisking. You can also use oil but it makes the cake taste slightly different, and it will be a little denser.

Sugar

You can use either granulated or soft brown sugar. The taste will change, but the texture should be the same.

Milk

You can use water—the results are about the same. The taste is a little different, but just as good. You can also use orange juice. The taste will be *very* different and the cake softer in texture.

Chocolate chips

You can use the same amount of anything you like: pieces of crystallized ginger, raisins, coconut, dates, even dried orange peel.

Helpful Hints

Cake too high on one side.
Either you put it at one side of the oven, or your oven heats unevenly.

Cake has a peak.
The hollow you made in the center was too shallow.

Cake has lumps of flour in it.
It needs more whisking. Be sure you touch the bottom of the bowl with every circle of the whisk through the mixture.

Cake doesn't rise at all.
Either the flour was old, or not real self-rising flour (it should say on the package), or you forgot the baking powder, if you used regular flour. However, the most likely reason is overbeating. (You can't make or take a phone call while making a cake and putting it in the oven. That guarantees you a home-baked frisbee.)

Cake has a black bottom.
The oven heat coming from the bottom is too hot, or the shelf is placed too low in the oven.

Cake rises over pan, and has holes in it.
It only happens if you use both self-rising flour *and* baking powder. (If your dog will eat it, fine, otherwise it's for the birds.) The cake will taste awful.

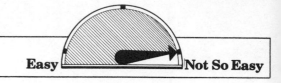

Easy ———— Not So Easy

Coffee Cake Rolls

This snack is not a quick one to make. In fact, unless you leave the dough out before you go to school, it can take longer than you might be prepared to wait. So plan ahead, and don't miss out on a super-snack.

Servings: 12 rolls.

Equipment

baking pan (approximately 12×9×2)

1-cup measure

paper towels

sharp knife

Ingredients

1 package frozen dough for making pizza

a little oil for your hands

1 cup sugar

1 teaspoon ground cinnamon

½ cup golden raisins

1 pat butter

Directions

1. You need one roll of dough. If the package has two, remember to thaw only one. Follow the directions on the package for thawing. You must follow these directions closely. If it says thaw at room temperature for four hours, or thereabouts, you can thaw the dough inside the refrigerator overnight or for a day, but that's all.

2. Preheat the oven to 425°F.

3. Press the dough out into a large rectangle with your hands slightly oiled. Keep working at it, it creeps back together unless you are really firm with it.

4. Once you have it rolled out, mix the sugar and the cinnamon together.

5. Sprinkle all the sugar and cinnamon mixture over the dough.

6. Then the raisins.

7. Roll the dough tightly into a long tube, starting with the short end.

8. Grease the baking pan with the butter using the paper towel.

9. Cut the long roll into twelve pieces. Do this carefully so that the shape is preserved.

10. Place the pieces in the pan.

11. Let them rise until double (approximately 15-30 mins.).

12. Place them in the oven to bake for thirty minutes, or until golden brown.

Substitutes

Dough

Some of the *bread* doughs work and some do not. The rolls will taste fine, but they sometimes will come out a bit hard and leathery. If you have never used frozen or refrigerated dough, use pizza dough. Otherwise use the dough you or your folks usually buy.

Filling

If you use brown sugar, use only about ½ cup packed down. Stir it up to loosen it for mixing with the cinnamon and for sprinkling.

Dark raisins work too. Dates do not. But if your market has the little date squares that are covered in sugar, they would work. But cut down the sugar in the recipe by ¼ cup.

Helpful Hints

As mentioned in **Substitutes**, some bread doughs work fine for this recipe and some do not. Often this has to do with temperature. All foods need temperatures which are best suited to them for taste, appearance, and health.

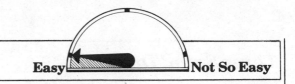

Three Salad Dressings

Any one of the following three salad dressings can be used with any one of the Three Salads with Raw Vegetables (see page 37). Or, as a matter of fact, with a salad of your invention.

Servings: 2 to 3 cups.

Equipment

1-cup measure

blender

big spoon for mixing

1-tablespoon measure

2-quart bowl

paper towels

I. Tomato and Mayonnaise Dressing

Ingredients

1 16-ounce can crushed tomatoes

1 cup mayonnaise

Directions

1. Put the tomatoes and mayonnaise in a 2-quart bowl and mix well before pouring on the salad.

II. Basil Dressing

Ingredients

1 cup mayonnaise

1 cup yogurt

1 small bunch fresh basil (about 6 stalks)

Directions

1. Be sure to wash the basil and pat dry between layers of paper towels.

2. Put the basil and other ingredients into the blender and turn on at high speed for a few seconds. This mixes the dressing and chops up the basil at the same time. (You can use the basil stems if they are not too thick.)

III. Russian Dressing

Ingredients

1 cup mayonnaise

1 cup yogurt

½ cup ketchup

½ cup sweet relish

2 tablespoons prepared mustard

Directions

1. Put all the ingredients into a 2-quart bowl and mix well before pouring on the salad.

Substitutes

You can use any of your favorite sauces or dressings. Remember they have to be thick so that all the food is coated and flavored. A runny dressing coats, but drips off without adding enough flavor to the salad.

Nutrition Notes

For a good salad to be a complete meal it must provide plenty of protein. Protein is often called the "body builder" because it helps you grow. Meats, fish, eggs, milk, and cheese are the main (or animal) proteins. Plants have protein too. The clue of the high-protein part of plants is the part that "grows" a new plant: the seed. In beans and peas (or legumes as scientists call them), the actual bean or pea is the seed. In nuts, the inner edible part is the seed. (Have you ever heard them called "nutmeats"?) In grains, the whole grain is the seed: the oat grain, the wheat grain, the barley grain, and the like.

There are many differences between animal and plant proteins, but from the point of view of the healthy eater, the main difference is that animal proteins are complete in themselves. To get a complete plant protein you have to mix and match foods from three groups: legumes, nuts, and grains.

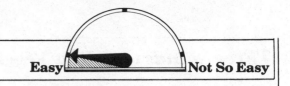
Three Salads with Raw Vegetables

Salad to many people is simply a collection of green leaves—called rabbit food. But rabbits have to have green leaves. We don't. We like, and need, variety. The more variety the better for our health. Here are three salads that have absolutely no lettuce in them. (Who needs a recipe to make a lettuce salad!) These salads are for lunches or to make for take-out meals, such as potluck dinners, church suppers, and the like.

Servings: 4 to 8 portions.

Equipment

large salad bowl (for each salad)

2 big spoons (or a salad fork and spoon) for tossing

knife for chopping

1-quart pot

2-quart pot

slotted spoon (to remove eggs from hot water)

vegetable peeler

grater

chopping board

Three Salads with Raw Vegetables

Basic Ingredient List for the Three Salads

In the three salads you will want to use a combination of at least three of the following vegetables. You will need about ½ pound per salad. The vegetables should be cut or snipped into bite-size pieces.

Canned artichoke hearts (drained)
Broccoli florets
Cauliflower florets
Celery
Canned corn (drained)

Fresh peas
Green or yellow squash
Green peppers
Spring onions or scallions
Tomatoes

I.   Potato and Egg Salad

Ingredients

4 large potatoes

4 hard-boiled eggs

Directions

1. Scrub the potatoes (of course, you can peel them if you want to).

2. Cut each potato into 4 pieces.

3. Put them into the 2-quart pot.

4. Cover the potatoes with water.

5. Boil them for 20 minutes. (If you want them softer, boil them longer.)

6. While the potatoes are cooking, put the eggs into the 1-quart pot half filled with cold water.

7. Over high heat, bring the water to a boil.

8. Boil the eggs for 10 minutes.

9. Remove the eggs from the boiling water with a big spoon and put them in the sink. Turn off the heat.

10. Run cold water over the eggs for about 5 minutes. You can peel them now or put them in cold water and peel later.

11. After the potatoes are cooked and cooled, cut them into cubes.

12. Slice the hard-boiled eggs.

13. Put the cubed potatoes and sliced eggs into the salad bowl.

14. Add whatever vegetables from the Basic Ingredient List you want.

15. Toss gently, using one of the following three salad dressings: tomato and mayonnaise, basil, or Russian (see pages 33-36).

II.   Macaroni and Ham Salad

Ingredients

1 large carrot

½ pound macaroni

½ pound cooked ham

Directions

1. Peel and shred the carrot into the salad bowl.

2. Cut the ham into squares and add to the salad bowl.

3. Cook the macaroni according to the directions on the box or package. (You can use any shape macaroni you want.)

4. Add the macaroni to the salad bowl after it has cooled.

5. Add whatever vegetables from the Basic Ingredient List you want.

6. Toss gently, using one of the following three salad dressings: tomato and mayonnaise, basil, or Russian (see pages 33-36).

III. Tortellini Salad

Tortellini is round pasta and is sometimes filled with cheese or meat.

Ingredients

1-pound package of tortellini (frozen or dried, filled or unfilled)

Directions

1. Cook the tortellini according to the directions on the box or package.

2. After the tortellini is cooled, put it in the salad bowl.

3. Add whatever vegetables from the Basic Ingredient List you want.

4. Toss gently, using one of the following three salad dressings: tomato and mayonnaise, basil, or Russian (see pages 33-36).

Substitutes

Salads

You can put almost anything in a salad. Cooked ground beef goes well with the tomato dressing; cooked and diced chicken or turkey goes well with the basil dressing.

You can use any shape of pasta. You can also use cooked rice, cooked bulgur wheat (crushed wheat), or a combination of these.

A delicious vegetarian salad can be made by combining rice, chick-peas and sunflower seeds with raw vegetables and any of the dressings on pages 33-36. (The reason for choosing rice, chick-peas, and sunflower seeds is because combined they make a better protein.)

Vegetables

All of the suggested vegetables can be eaten raw. They are delicious and taste different from cooked vegetables. Be sure to wash them well and gently pat dry with a paper towel. If the list of vegetables does not have your favorites, then make up your own list. All the vegetables can be substituted with 1½ pounds of drained, canned corn, but try for a mixture of at least 3 vegetables. They taste *much* better that way—promise.

Easy ◤ Not So Easy

Mexican Crunch Lunch

This recipe can be made ahead of time, or made just before you want to serve it by browning the meat first, and putting it in the refrigerator to chill while you prepare the remainder of the ingredients. If you have never eaten Mexican food, this is a good recipe to start with. The flavors and textures are not *too* foreign. If you love Mexican food, but don't like it too spicy, this is also a good recipe for you because you can control the spice level. It's called a crunch lunch because it has crunchy tortilla chips in it.

Servings: 4 hearty portions.

Equipment

frying pan

spatula

1-teaspoon measure

3- or 4-quart bowl

chopping board

knife for chopping

serving spoon and fork

¼-cup measure

½-cup measure

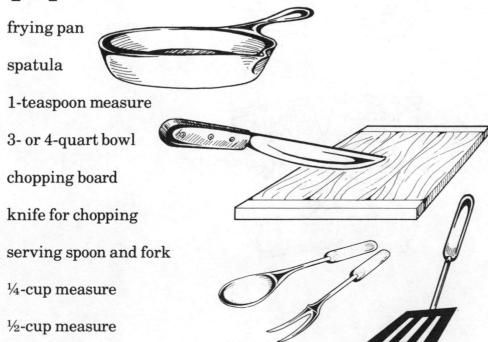

Ingredients

1 pound ground beef

½ teaspoon each of chili powder, cumin, garlic flakes, and oregano

1 16-ounce can red kidney beans

1 medium onion

2 green peppers

1 avocado

1 large tomato

½ pound cheddar cheese

¼ cup salad oil

½ cup vinegar

1-pound package tortilla chips

Directions

1. Brown the ground beef in the frying pan over high heat for about 5 minutes, then lower the heat and cook slowly until done. Make sure the meat is separated by chopping it gently with the side of the spatula while it cooks. After the meat is browned, turn off the heat.

2. Stir in the chili powder, cumin, garlic flakes, and oregano. Mix well.

3. Put the spiced and cooked meat mixture into the bowl and put it in the refrigerator to chill. You can cover it with a plate, plastic bag, or foil paper.

4. While the mixture is chilling, open the can of beans and drain them.

5. Peel the onion.

6. Slice the green peppers in half lengthwise (be sure to clean out the seeds).

7. Cut the avocado in half and peel it.

8. Cut the tomato and the other vegetables into cubes.

9. Next, cut the cheddar cheese into cubes, too.

10. Take the spiced meat mixture out of the refrigerator and add the oil and vinegar. Mix until the oil and vinegar look absorbed.

11. Add the vegetables, including the beans, and the cheese and toss gently with the serving spoon and fork.

12. Crumble about half the tortilla chips to make them smaller. Add them into the mixture.

Continued

13. Arrange the remainder of the chips around the edge before serving. (If you are not going to serve this lunch right away, do not add the tortilla chips. They should be added just before serving or they will get very soggy.)

Substitutes

Meat
You can make this recipe with a can of chili, or a sloppy joe mix used with ground meat. It's a good way to use up leftover chili, too.

Vegetables
You can add other vegetables. Corn, for example, goes well with this recipe, but the combination in the recipe tastes the best. Some cooks may like to use more fresh onion; others may prefer scallions instead.

Tortilla chips
It depends on your favorite brand, but the recipe tastes best with either taco-flavored corn chips or nacho cheese tortilla chips.

Potato chips don't work too well, and any other similar snacks spoil the flavor (cheese doodles, for instance, *ruin* it).

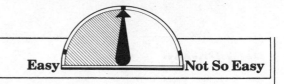
Pita Power

This recipe is for a filling to put into neat little bread pockets called pita bread (also called Sahara bread). Pitas are circles of bread piled together like a stack of saucers, and each is about as thick as a saucer. This kind of pita can be made into pockets, which is the kind you need for this recipe.

Servings: enough to generously fill 8 moderately large pita pockets.

Equipment

large bowl

baking pan (about 15×9×2)

knife for chopping

chopping board

pair kitchen scissors

blender

tablespoon

1-teaspoon measure

½-cup measure

¼-cup measure

paper towel

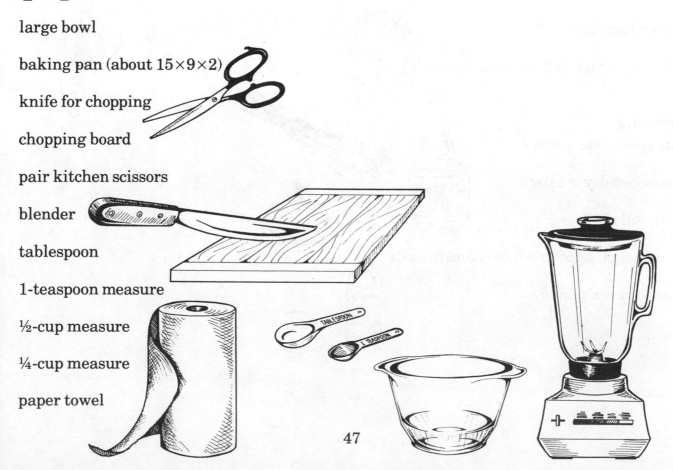

47

Ingredients

1 packet of 8 pita pockets

1 pound ground beef

1 package dry onion soup mix

½ cup water

1 small head lettuce

1 large tomato

1 medium onion or 1 bunch scallions

Dressing

1 teaspoon celery seeds

1 teaspoon dry mustard

¼ cup salad oil

½ cup lemon juice (fresh or reconstituted)

1 large bunch parsley

Directions

1. Preheat oven to 375°F. Be sure there is a middle shelf in the oven.

2. Mix the ground beef, the onion soup mix, and ½ cup of water in the bowl until they make a fairly thorough mixture.

3. Shape the mixture into 8 patties.

4. Put them on the baking pan.

5. Bake for about 25 minutes. While the patties are baking, do steps 6 through 11.

6. Cut across the top of each pita; and then, with your fingers, loosen the inside gently to make a pocket. Set aside.

7. Shred the lettuce.

8. Chop the tomato into slices or cubes.

9. Snip the scallions with scissors. (If you use an onion, slice it as thin as possible or cut up into tiny pieces.)

10. Take the leaves off the parsley. You can use a bit of the stalks, but not much. Wash the parsley leaves and pat dry with paper towel.

11. Put all the dressing ingredients in the blender at "chop" setting and blend until the parsley is chopped. Be sure the blender lid fits securely.

12. After the ground beef has baked for 25 minutes, turn off the oven. Stuff the pita pockets with some lettuce, a meat patty, some more lettuce, some tomato, and some onion, then hold it upright and pour a tablespoonful of dressing into the pocket. Eat carefully!

Substitutes

Pita
You can choose whole wheat or white pitas.

Meat
You can use sloppy joe mix or a can of chili. These need to be heated. If you are in a real rush you can use them cold, but they taste better heated. You can add the following to get a spicier flavor:

¼ teaspoon ground coriander
¼ teaspoon ground cumin
¼ teaspoon garlic flakes

If it does not taste spicy enough, you can double the amounts, but *never more* than double for the quantities given.

Vegetables
These are the vegetables mostly used, but you could add your favorites. And some people even add 2 tablespoons of plain yogurt to each pita.

Dressing
You can use the chick-pea and sesame seed dip on page 23.

Helpful Hints

Pita pockets are better if you can warm them first. Don't try the toaster, though, it just burns the edges and does not warm the whole pita. Put them in the oven at about 300°F for 5 or 6 minutes.

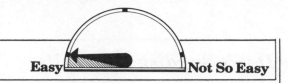
Dan's Swedish Meatballs

You may not be as surprised at the combination of ingredients in this recipe as your folks, but you can assure them that grape jelly, chili sauce, and ground beef taste just great together.

Servings: about 4 meatballs each (the size of golf balls) for 4 people.

Equipment

frying pan

large pot (3- or 4-quart)

wooden spoon

Ingredients

1 pound ground meat

1 8-ounce jar grape jelly

1 16-ounce jar chili sauce

Directions

1. Put the frying pan on the burner over low heat.

2. Place the ground meat on the countertop.

3. Using your hands divide the meat down the middle into 2 pieces.

4. Then divide each of the 2 pieces down the middle.

5. Keep doing this until you get 16 little pieces of ground meat all about the same size.

6. Gently shape the pieces of meat into a round ball the size of a golf ball and put them one at a time into the frying pan.

7. After all the meatballs are in the pan turn the heat up to brown them. Don't use the highest heat setting or the meatballs will burn and stick. You don't want to cook them, just brown them on the outside.

8. Keep turning the round balls gently so they get brown all over.

9. While you are doing this, you can put the large pot on another burner over low heat.

10. Pour all the contents of the jar of jelly and the jar of chili sauce into the pot.

11. Heat slowly while you are browning the meatballs.

12. After the meatballs are brown all over, turn off the heat. Put the meatballs in the pot with the jelly and chili sauce.

13. Let them simmer for about 20 minutes over low heat. Turn off the heat.

Substitutes

Meat

You can use any kind of meat in this recipe. Hot Italian sausage makes a wild and wonderful dish. Ground lamb is good, and so is ground veal or pork (cook the pork about 10 minutes longer in the pot) or even a mixture of several kinds of ground meat.

Sauce

There really is no substitute for the sauce because that's what makes this dish. You can, however, get another type of sweet-and-peppery sauce by using chili sauce, a small jar of apricot jam, and 1 teaspoonful of ground ginger. (Certain Eastern recipes use this apricot-and-ginger combination, so you might call the recipe "Oriental meatballs.")

Helpful Hints

To make this a meal, you really need a green vegetable and a potato. A salad would be the easiest since it doesn't need cooking (see page 37). Instead of a potato, you could cook rice, which is often served with meatballs. Or a package of instant cracked wheat (cous-cous). Follow the directions on the package to make the quantity you want. The reason cous-cous is so good with this dish is because it's bland, which helps the flavor of the sauce. It's chewy and grainy like rice, but tastes different and is a pleasant change from rice. You could also try bulgur wheat, or brown rice. If you don't feel that adventurous, this dish goes really well with mashed potatoes (and even just bread instead of potatoes).

Nutrition Note

Worried about all that jelly? Think it's too much sugar? It's about the same amount of jelly as some people put on one fat peanut butter-and-jelly sandwich. Still worried? Ok, cut the amount of jelly in half. It's still a delicious dish.

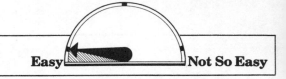
Mini Steak Dinner

Steak got its name from the "stake" used to cook the slabs of meat over fire. It's a thick slice of meat or perhaps fish: ham steak, swordfish steak, beefsteak.

This mini steak dinner is not only delicious, but also filling.

Servings: 4 portions.

Equipment

tablespoon

small pot

frying pan

pair of tongs (or a spatula)

Ingredients

1 10-ounce can condensed mushroom soup

4 beefsteaks, cubed (about 1½ pounds)

Directions

1. Pour the contents of the soup can into the pot. You may have to scrape it out of the can with a tablespoon because it's *very* thick when it's cold.

2. Put the soup pot on the burner over a low heat. Stir from time to time to prevent sticking.

3. Put the frying pan on another burner at a high temperature. (A slow count to 5 for gas or 15 for electric is enough to heat the frying pan.)

4. Put the 4 steaks into the pan. These steaks cook very quickly, so watch closely. As soon as you see a slight hint of gray color at the edges (about 1 to 2 minutes), turn the steaks very carefully with the tongs or the spatula.

5. Give the steaks 1 to 2 minutes on the other side. Turn the heat off.

6. Pour the hot mushroom sauce (the soup) over the steaks in the frying pan.

7. Move the meat around a little in the sauce to pick up the meat brownings from the bottom of the pan. Serve immediately.

Substitutes

Meat

This recipe works with any kind of ground meat patties (hamburger, veal, lamb). It also works nicely with chicken breasts, but you need to cook them longer (see page 58). You can also use fish steak. It doesn't taste too good if you use ham, however, because the salt in the ham combined with the salt in the soup adds up to one very salty dish!

Mushroom sauce

Cream of tomato soup works fine. You could make your own sauce from almost any soup you like, except cream of celery soup, which is a real loser in this recipe.

You could also make white sauce (see page 76), and dilute it with 1 cup of beef broth, or tomato juice, or 1 cup of milk and 1 cup of mushroom pieces.

Helpful Hints

A green salad (see page 37) and a roll make this a very quick meal. Some mashed potatoes and a green vegetable of your choice will take more time to fix, but will be more nutritious, and more filling.

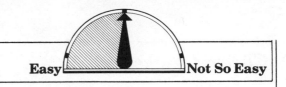
Cheesy Chicken

This is a quick and an easy recipe. You'll come back to it time and again because it's so good (although some people may think the combination of flavors—cheese and chicken—a little unusual).

Servings: 2 moderate portions, or 1 large one.

Equipment

baking pan about 12×9×2 (if you double the recipe you may need to double the size of the pan)

piece of foil slightly larger than the baking pan

pair kitchen scissors

Ingredients

1 10-ounce package of frozen cauliflower-and-cheese

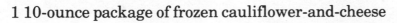

2 skinless and boneless chicken breasts (about ½ pound each)

Directions

1. Take the frozen package of cauliflower-and-cheese out of the freezer about half an hour before you start.

2. Preheat the oven to 375°F. Be sure there is a middle shelf in the oven.

3. Lay each breast of chicken in the baking pan close together, but not touching, with the top side up. (The top side is the smooth side.)

4. Open the package of cauliflower-and-cheese. If there's an inside plastic pouch, snip that open too.

5. Break the thawed cauliflower-and-cheese in half and put half on top of each chicken breast.

6. Put the foil over the pan of chicken and cauliflower-and-cheese.

7. Press the foil over the edges of the pan to seal it.

8. Then very carefully poke 4 small holes in the corners of the foil with your fingers. This allows the steam to escape.

9. Place the pan in the oven and bake for 20 minutes.

Substitutes

Chicken
You can use fillets of fish instead of the chicken breasts: sole, haddock, in fact any white, nonoily fish. It still takes one fillet cut in half for 2 people, with 1 package of the cauliflower-and-cheese sauce. Make sure the fish fillet weighs about 8 to 10 ounces. If it has a thin tail, or if you get 2 small fillets, tuck the thin end under. This way the thin portion is doubled over and won't cook too fast and burn. Check the market for frozen inexpensive small shrimp and use them frozen.

Vegetables
There are lots of vegetable-and-cheese sauce combinations on the market. Broccoli seems a natural, and looks very good with white fish or chicken, or pink shrimp. Vegetable-haters may prefer the cauliflower because the broccoli flavor can be slightly stronger and cover up the chicken or fish flavor.

Helpful Hints

A green salad (see page 37), and popovers (see page 17), or garlic bread (see page 20) would make this a complete meal.

59

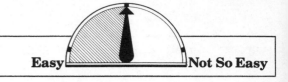

Easy | Not So Easy

Lemon Chicken

This is often called piccata (pick-ah-tah). If it is made with small thin circles of veal (called escallopes), it will appear on menus as *veal piccata*. Chicken versions appear often on menus, too, but not with such fancy names. However, lemon chicken tastes delicious, and is a quick dish to make.

Servings: 4 portions.

Equipment

pair kitchen scissors

frying pan

spatula

dinner plate

Ingredients

2 whole skinless and boneless chicken breasts

¼ stick butter or margarine

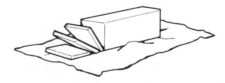

½ cup lemon juice (fresh or reconstituted)

Directions

1. Use the scissors to cut each breast in half (this will give you 4 pieces of chicken). There may be a center piece of gristly breastbone left. Use the scissors to cut this out completely and discard it.

2. Cut each piece of breast into about 5 pieces of roughly the same size.

3. Melt the butter or margarine in the frying pan over moderate heat. Place the pieces of chicken side by side in the butter. You can place them quite close together because they will shrink in cooking. All the chicken should fit into the frying pan.

4. Let the chicken simmer in the butter for about 10 minutes. It's ready to turn when you can see that the sides have turned the white color of cooked chicken.

5. Turn the chicken pieces over carefully with the spatula and let them cook for another 10 minutes. If the pieces have stuck together in cooking, separate them gently with the edge of the spatula.

6. After the chicken is cooked, transfer it to the plate. Most of the butter will be left in the pan together with some chicken juices.

7. Add all the lemon juice to the pan, turn the heat up to high, and stir the sauce gently until it boils. If there is a brownish color to the sauce, that comes from the browned chicken juices in the pan. It's delicious. Generally, though, because of the amount of butter, the chicken does not get browned in cooking, so the sauce is a creamy color. As it boils, the sauce thickens a bit.

8. Put the chicken back in the pan and turn the pieces in the sauce. Turn the heat off.

9. Put the chicken back on the plate and pour remaining sauce over it before it's served.

Substitutes

Chicken
Veal, any white fish, shrimp, scallops, or lobster pieces can be used in place of chicken.

Sauce
There is not much possibility here for variety. Orange or lime juice would work quite well, except many people are not used to such a combination of flavors. You could use any juice, really, to get the tangy flavor. If, however, the juice is colored, such as grape or cranberry juice, the chicken will turn a strange and unappetizing color. Many people don't know it, but we eat with our eyes almost as much as with our mouths. If you don't like the look of a food, you sometimes won't even give it a try!

Nutrition Note

Chicken has so little vitamin C that this recipe pleases nutritionists because the lemon juice adds vitamin C to the chicken so you get a more nutritious helping of the vitamin.

Easy ▲ Not So Easy

Oven Lasagna

One of the problems of cooking lasagna is layering the hot pasta strips. This recipe helps to avoid this problem by cooking the lasagna pasta along with the other ingredients. It takes about the same amount of time, and it tastes just as good.

Servings: 4 large (or 6 moderate) portions.

Equipment

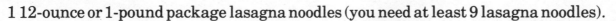

baking pan (about 15×9×2)

spatula

piece of foil slightly larger than the baking pan

Ingredients

1 12-ounce or 1-pound package lasagna noodles (you need at least 9 lasagna noodles).

1 2-pound jar homestyle spaghetti sauce

1 pound ricotta cheese

4 slices mozarella cheese

Directions

1. Preheat the oven to 400°F. Be sure there is a middle shelf in the oven.

2. Put a layer of sauce in the bottom of the pan.

3. Spread 3 lasagna noodles on top of the sauce so they lie side by side and cover the entire bottom of the pan. (Break the noodles to fit if you have bought large noodles or are using a different size pan.)

4. Using the spatula, spread about one-third of the ricotta cheese over the noodles. (You may have to use your fingers to hold the noodles in place while you do this.)

5. Cover the ricotta cheese with more sauce.

6. Add a second layer of noodles.

7. Spread the noodles with ricotta cheese as in step number 4.

8. Cover the second layer of ricotta cheese with sauce.

9. Then spread the third, and last, layer of noodles on top.

10. By this time you have probably reached to nearly the top of the pan. If so, just spread the last of the ricotta cheese on top of the last layer of noodles.

11. The last step is to cover with sauce. (If your pan is smaller and deeper, you will need to make smaller but more layers. If your pan is larger and shallower, you may need to make one layer less.)

12. Once the pan is full, cover it with the foil. Press the foil over the edges of the pan to seal it.

13. Put in the oven and bake for 45 minutes.

14. Take it out of the oven and remove the foil very carefully.

15. Place the 4 slices of mozarella cheese on top. Put it back in the oven, uncovered, for 15 minutes or until the cheese melts. Turn off the oven. Serve while hot.

Substitutes

Cheese

You can use layers of mozarella cheese between the sauce along with the ricotta cheese if you like. It makes the lasagna cheesier. It also makes it "stringy" after it's cooked. You can partly avoid this by letting the dish "set" for about 10 minutes after it is cooked.

You can substitute white American cheese in place of the mozarella if you like. It behaves differently in the recipe, but looks almost like the real thing.

Sauce

Marinara sauce (a tomato sauce with herbs or spices but no meat) is also very good in this recipe. You can add chopped up vegetables to the sauce if you like. Or you can use a 1-pound jar of spaghetti sauce, and a 1-pound can of chopped tomatoes. Combine them before spreading them on the cheese and pasta.

Plain tomato sauce works as well, but needs to be spiced up for this recipe: Use 2 teaspoons of Italian herbs. (It comes already mixed in a little jar that you can usually find in the spice and herb rack at the market.)

Helpful Hints

This is an easy recipe if you have exactly the right size of pan, one that matches the size of the lasagna you buy. The directions on the lasagna package tell you what to do if your pans are too small or too shallow. However, if you don't have exactly the right pan, the best alternatives are either two 8-inch square cake pans, or a moderate size (about 20×10) roasting pan. Try not to have any leftover sauce because it doesn't keep as long as uncooked leftover lasagna.

A green salad with this dish makes it into a full meal (see page 37). But why not try something a little different, say, a fruit cup to start with? The pasta takes the place of potato. And green beans or peas make a nice color contrast and go well with the dish if you want a vegetable.

Nutrition Note

Remember: Enriched pasta products are better for you, so check the labels when you shop.

Quick Barbecued Chicken

This recipe is called quick barbecue because it is not necessary to stand over it turning and basting. The sauce itself is enough to baste the meat. And the meat is chicken with the bone still in it so that you can, if allowed to, eat it with your fingers.

Servings: 4 portions.

Equipment

Electric frying pan
or
casserole that can be used in the oven (about 10×8×4)

4-cup measure

1-tablespoon measure

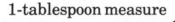

1-teaspoon measure

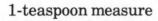

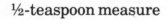

½-teaspoon measure

Quick Barbecued Chicken

Ingredients

1 package chicken thighs or drumsticks (about 1½ pounds)

¼ cup packed brown sugar

½ cup ketchup

¼ cup vinegar

2 tablespoons Worcestershire sauce

1 tablespoon prepared mustard

½ teaspoon dried minced garlic

1 teaspoon dried minced onion

½ teaspoon celery seed

½ teaspoon hot chili powder

1 16-ounce can tomato sauce

Directions

1. Open the package of chicken and arrange in the casserole or the electric frying pan. If you are using an oven, preheat the oven to 375°F. Be sure there is a middle shelf in the oven.

2. Using the 4-cup measure, pack the brown sugar to the ½ cup mark.

3. Then slowly pour in the ketchup to the ¾ cup mark.

4. Next, slowly pour in the vinegar to the 1 cup mark. (You must do it in this order because the ketchup protects the sugar from dissolving in the vinegar until the pouring is finished.)

5. Add to this the 2 tablespoons of Worcestershire sauce.

6. Then, using the same spoon, add the mustard. Stir a bit with the tablespoon to get all the mustard off of it.

7. Then add the rest of the spices—garlic, onion, celery seed, chili powder—and stir well.

8. Add the tomato sauce.

9. Stir gently because at this point the 4-cup measure is getting rather full.

10. Pour the barbecue mixture over the chicken.

11. Put the dish in the oven. If you are using an electric frying pan, put the lid on. Plug the pan in after you have added the sauce. Set the control to 300°F.

12. The chicken has to cook for at least 45 minutes, but it can go for about 30 minutes longer to make it even tastier or until the meat starts to fall off the bones into the sauce. Remember: turn off the oven or unplug the electric frying pan.

Substitutes

Chicken
This barbecue sauce can be used with many foods. It makes a great sloppy joe if you add ground meat. If you use an 8-ounce (instead of a 16-ounce) can of tomato sauce along with the other ingredients, you have a tasty sauce for baked ham. If you add 2 cups of water and an 8-ounce can of beans and 2 frozen packages of your favorite vegetables, you have a humdinger of a soup. (Beets and spinach make the soup taste good but they give it a rather unusual appearance.)

Sauce
You can use a can of sloppy joe, or a can of chili. You can even mix a can of tomato sauce with a can of ravioli (or other pasta). It's not really barbecued chicken, but it's a good chicken casserole.

Helpful Hints

The oven temperature can be set at 300°F, so you can leave this dish in for a maximum of 2½ hours.

A great favorite with this dish is hot biscuits, especially for dunkers. The sauce seems to me made for dunking—biscuits, bread, crispy rolls, soft rolls, and the like.

Also, a crisp crunchy salad is great with this meal (see page 37).

If you add a package of frozen peas at the end, and put it back in the oven for 20 minutes, you've got a one-dish meal. (If you find the peas are not cooked soft enough for your taste, give the casserole 10 minutes more in the oven.)

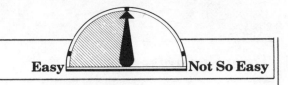

Taco Surprises

A taco is mostly ground cornmeal shaped like a small plate. It is the Mexican version of a pancake much like the French pancake, or *crepe*. (Not the doughy kind of pancake we eat with butter and syrup for breakfast.) It is crisp. There is a soft Mexican "pancake" also made of cornmeal, but it's called a *tortilla*. Tacos don't taste like "corn chips." They are prepared differently, and have a flavor all their own. Cornmeal prepared this way is one of the wonderful flavors of Mexican cooking.

Servings: 12 tacos.

Equipment

baking pan (about 12×9×2)

knife for chopping

chopping board

tablespoon

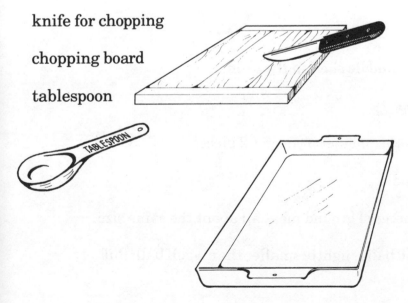

Ingredients

2 pounds ground chuck beef

2 large tomatoes

1 large green pepper

1 small head lettuce

1 8-ounce package of any kind of grated cheese

1 package 12 taco shells

1 bottle *mild* taco sauce

Directions

1. Preheat oven to 375°F. Be sure there is a middle shelf in the oven.

2. Place the ground meat on the countertop.

3. Using your hands divide the meat down the middle so you get 2 pieces.

4. Divide each of the 2 pieces down the middle.

5. Keep doing this until you get 24 little pieces of ground meat all about the same size.

6. Gently mold the pieces of meat into round balls slightly smaller than a golf ball. Put them one at a time into the baking pan.

7. Once you have the 24 meatballs in the baking pan, put them in the oven to cook for 20 minutes.

72

8. While the little meatballs are cooking, chop the tomatoes, peppers and lettuce. The lettuce should be sliced into long shreds. Cut the pepper lengthwise in half, remove the center with seeds, and then cut each half in slices. Halve the tomato, then quarter it. Next slice off the top where the stem was. Cut each quarter in slices (across is better than lengthwise, but both ways are messy). You now have 3 piles of vegetables to put into the tacos.

9. Open the package of grated cheese and loosen so it separates easily.

10. Open the package of tacos.

11. Take the meatballs from the oven. Turn the oven off.

12. Put a small bed of lettuce on the bottom of 1 taco.

13. Place 2 meatballs on top;
    then some tomato;
    some green pepper;
    and finish off with the grated cheese.

14. Serve with the taco sauce.

Repeat for the other tacos, or let everyone make his or her own.

Substitutes

Meatballs
Here are two other versions of spiced meat for taco filling:

1. Put the 2 pounds of meat in a 2 quart pot and brown over high heat. Stir the meat with a wooden spoon to break it up and to expose it evenly over the heat. Add 1 can or package of sloppy joe mix, stir well, bring to boil, and then lower the heat to a simmer for 20 minutes.

2. Brown the meat as above over high heat. Add a teaspoonful of chili powder, 2 teaspoons of dry minced onion, ½ teaspoon of dry minced garlic, ½ teaspoon of ground cumin, ¼ teaspoon of dried oregano, ¼ teaspoon of celery seeds. Stir the mixture well. Add 1 cup of water, stir well, bring to boil. Lower the heat and simmer 2 minutes. This produces a mild flavor. For that "five-alarm" flavor, double the spices and add 1 teaspoon of hot sauce (*Tabasco*).

Sauce
The sauce is mild, because most people like it that way. You can also buy a hot taco sauce. Or you can use the mild sauce with a chili sauce on the side. Or you can mix equal quantities of ketchup and hot chili sauce for a milder, equally good taco sauce if you don't like the flavor of the sauces. Check the market to see if it has an avocado salad dressing—this can make a wild taco topping.

Helpful Hints

Tacos are supposed to be crisp and crunchy. If you bought a package that turns out to be soft, there are two things you can do.

1. Check the label to see if you bought tacos that need some sort of cooking or heating. If so, follow the instructions carefully.
2. Put the oven on before you do anything else, and while it is heating, place the soft tacos on a tray on the middle shelf of the oven for a few minutes. When you take them out (do not let them get browner) they will still seem a little soft but will become crisp while cooling. These recipes are for mild sauces. If you feel brave, or are used to hot spices, here's how to get a really hot sauce: Double all the spices listed above, and add 1 teaspoon of hot sauce (*Tabasco* is best).

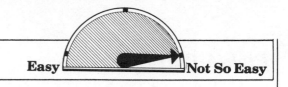

Easy | Not So Easy

Pick-A-Puff

This is a twofold recipe. First is an all-purpose white sauce. Second is puff pastry. Why is it called Pick-a-Puff? Because YOU choose what you want to go into the white sauce. And that combination is what fills up the pastry to give you a tasty treat.

Servings: 12 pastries.

Equipment

2-quart pot

1-cup measure

1-tablespoon measure

wax paper

whisk

2 cookie sheets (about 12×9×2)

rolling pin

knife for cutting

Ingredients

Sauce

¾ stick margarine

4 tablespoons flour

1 cup milk

Pastry

1 package frozen puff pastry dough

flour

Filling

1 cup chopped hard boiled eggs

or

1 cup chopped cooked meat or chicken

or

1 cup flaked cooked fish

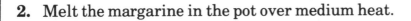

Directions

Sauce

1. Put the 4 tablespoons of flour onto a piece of wax paper.

2. Melt the margarine in the pot over medium heat.

3. Stir the margarine with the whisk so that the bottom of the pot is completely covered.

4. Add the flour all at once.

5. Stir the flour so it is well mixed with the margarine.

6. Cook for about 3 minutes. it will bubble a lot because there is more fat than flour. That's all right, just stir if it starts to separate. The most important thing is not to let the mixture get brown.

7. Next, pour in the cup of milk.

8. Stir the mixture well. Use the whisk like a spoon, stirring round and round to get all the fat/flour mixture off the bottom of the pot.

9. Once it's all floating in lumps in the milk, start to gently whisk it. The lumps should dissolve with the whisking and the heating of the milk. As this happens the sauce starts to thicken.

10. As the bubbles start to plop up through the thick sauce, showing that it's boiling, use the whisk as a spoon once again, and stir vigorously for 2 minutes while it boils. And there you have it: an all-purpose white sauce.

Pastry

11. Put one of the cookie sheets on the bottom shelf of the oven.

12. Preheat the oven to 425°F.

13. Let the pastry thaw according to the directions on the package. Do not let it thaw too long or it will get really messy and stick to everything.

14. Sprinkle a little flour on the countertop and put the pastry on it. (If there are 2 pieces in your package, deal with them one at a time.)

15. Cut the pastry into 3 long strips (there may be fold-lines to guide you).

16. Take a strip and, using the rolling pin, roll the strip lengthwise until it is twice its length.

17. Cut the strip in half.

18. Do this to the other 2 strips. You now have 6 strips of pastry.

19. Repeat this with the second sheet of pastry. You now have 12 strips of pastry.

20. Mix the 1 cup of filling with the thick white sauce.

21. Place 2 to 3 tablespoons of the filling on the end of one of the pastry strips. Fold the other end of the pastry over the filled end.

Continued

22. Pinch the edges together. If you don't pinch hard, the filling may fall out.

23. Place the pastry on the second cookie sheet.

24. Put the cookie sheet in the preheated oven on the bottom shelf for 20 minutes, or until the pastry turns a golden-brown color and looks puffy.

25. It's too hot to eat immediately, so let it cool off a bit. Turn off the oven.

Substitutes

Pastry

A plain pastry or packaged frozen pie crust works well for this recipe.

You can make the puff pastry in muffin cups, too. Place very carefully in the muffin pan the 12 pieces of pastry you prepared from the directions. Try not to stretch the pastry—if it tears it will not puff too well. A rim of pastry will hang over onto the flat surface of the muffin pan. This is fine because it makes little "ears" that can help you take the muffins out after they're cooked.

Filling

Meats. Any cooked meat that is chopped fairly small is good. Ham and chicken work best. You can use kitchen scissors to cut up the meat.

Fish. Cooked fish is good. Flake it into small pieces with your fingers. Shrimp are also tasty.

Eggs. Chopped hard-boiled eggs are tasty in this recipe. Try them with a few chopped olives for a treat (if you like olives).

Vegetables. Peas are best for color; corn is easiest because it needs no cooking. Avoid watery vegetables (tomatoes, cooked squash, cucumbers).

Salads. Tuna salad, chicken salad, and ham salad work best of all.

Helpful Hints

This is supposed to be a sure-fire sauce. White sauce, however, can be tricky. If you have a sauce that turns out a little lumpy, or the bottom feels as though it's sticking (and, oh horrors, perhaps burning) take the pot off the heat, and pour the sauce into a blender. Scrape most of the lumps off the bottom of the pan, leaving the brown bits, and give it about half-a-minute whiz in the blender. If it needs a touch more thickening, cook it for a few more minutes. Pour it back into the pot and stir well while it boils for 2 minutes. (Of course, you scrubbed any brown bits off the bottom first, didn't you?)

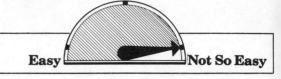
Shepherd's Pie

This pie is traditionally made with mutton, which is a dry meat that needs a sauce or gravy to go with it. Shepherd's pie works with any leftover roast meat. It also works very well with ground meat. This version, for simplicity, economy, and guaranteed results is made with ground beef. (Using leftovers, especially of roast meats, takes a great deal of skill and knowledge to get a result that is not dry and chewy.)

Servings: 4 portions.

Equipment

2-quart pot

frying pan

chopping board

knife for chopping

4-quart pot

wooden spoon

2-quart oven-proof casserole

spatula

Ingredients

1 cup milk

1 pound ground beef

2 medium onions

1 teaspoon celery seeds

2 tablespoons gravy browning (*Kitchen Bouquet*, for instance)

1 tablespoon Worcestershire sauce

1 24-ounce package frozen peas and carrots

1 cup water

¼ stick butter or margarine

2 cups instant potato flakes

Directions

1. Put the milk into the 2-quart pot over a very low heat.

2. Put the frying pan over a moderately high heat.

3. Pick the ground beef into small pieces with your fingers and put into the frying pan, turning the meat from time to time.

4. While the meat is browning, prepare the onions. Cut the skin off the onions. Then cut each one in half. Place the cut side down on the chopping board.

5. Cut about 4 slices across the onion one way, then cut about 4 or 5 slices the other way.

6. By the time you have finished preparing the onions the meat should be done. Put the meat in the 4-quart pot over a medium heat.

7. Fry the onions in the frying pan before you add them to the meat. (If you want them brown, fry them until they are done to your satisfaction. If you want them white but cooked, don't fry them for such a long time.) Turn off the heat.

8. Now add the celery seeds, gravy browning, and Worcestershire sauce to the meat and onions. Mix them in thoroughly.

9. Add the peas and carrots and the cup of water. Don't mix the vegetables into the meat just yet, leave them on top. This way, they cook in the steam from the water that is simmering the meat.

10. Put the lid on the pot and cook for 20 minutes.

11. The milk for the mashed potatoes should now be very hot—but not boiling.

12. Add the butter to the milk and stir until it melts.

13. Take the pot off the heat and stir in the potato flakes. Leave this to sit, with the lid on to keep it warm, until the meat is ready. Turn off the heat.

14. After the meat mixture is done, put it into the casserole and spread the mashed potato over it gently with the spatula.

15. Put the filled casserole under the broiler to brown slightly or sprinkle a little paprika over it to give it a touch of color.

Substitutes

Meat and vegetables
You can use almost any kind of meat you like in this recipe. If it's a ground meat, follow the same directions. If it's a piece of, say, chuck steak cut up into small pieces, the directions for browning would be the same, but you might find you need an extra 10 minutes cooking in the pot. Do this before you add the vegetables to cook for 20 minutes.

You can also use as many vegetables as you like: corn, parsnip, turnip, lima beans, and other starchy vegetables that need the same amount of time to cook as peas and carrots. (Cut them into small pieces.) Leafy vegetables, such as cabbage, spinach, brussels sprouts, for example, don't work.

Potato
You can make mashed potatoes from whole raw potatoes that you cook and then mash or from leftover cooked potatoes.

Helpful Hints

This is a rather complicated recipe. Recipes tend to get complicated when a lot of ingredients are involved, or when the directions assume you know something about cooking. For example, in this recipe the meat and vegetable mixture shouldn't end up with too much watery gravy, but sometimes it does. Some of the packages of frozen vegetables have more frost in them than others, or some vegetables contain more water than others.

What to do if this happens? Simple. Add about ¼ cup of instant potato flakes and quickly thicken up the sauce.

Some cooks do not like using potato flakes. And raw potato is possible in this recipe. Scrub the potatoes with a nylon scrub or vegetable brush (peel them if you want). Slice them. Layer the slices on top of the casserole. Cook the casserole in a moderate (375°F) oven for 45 minutes.

If you choose to use raw potatoes, don't cook the meat and vegetables on top of the stove. Put everything from the frying pan straight into the casserole; add the seasonings, vegetables, and water; mix them together and arrange the raw potato slices on top. You may want to dab the potato slices with butter.

Many recipes use the phrase "dot (or dab) with butter." There are two easy ways to do it. Use a butter knife and soft butter and simply spread a tiny portion of butter on each exposed potato slice. Second, faster but not as tidy, is to scoop up a large lump of butter on a clean finger and smear the whole potato topping gently with 2 or 3 long strokes.

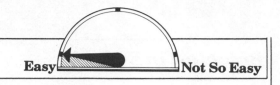
Breakfast in Bed

The nicest thing about having breakfast in bed is that you don't have to prepare it yourself. It makes one feel rather grand—all this fuss over the simplest meal of the day. So this recipe is not just for food—but it's a recipe for a mood, also.

Servings: one (for a special person).

Equipment

tray

coffee-making equipment

toaster

cloth or napkin to fit on tray

small orange juice glass

small jam dish or a saucer

small spoon for jam

small butter dish or a saucer

butter knife

small milk pitcher

small sugar bowl

cup and saucer

plate

oven-proof dish or shallow bowl

1 small towel or a clean napkin

Ingredients

coffee

sugar

milk

orange juice

toast

butter

jam

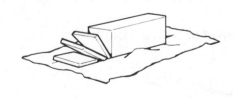

Directions

1. Start by making the coffee.

2. Put the cloth on the tray. If you do not have a tray, a sturdy cookie sheet or large baking pan can work just as well. If you do not have a cloth for the tray, use paper napkins, colored or white.

3. Set the tray with the orange juice; put a spoonful or two of jam on the jam dish or saucer; a pat or two of butter on the butter dish or saucer; sugar, if needed, and the milk pitcher.

4. Also set the tray with the cup and saucer, butter knife, napkin, and plate.

5. Run very hot water from the tap over the oven-proof dish until it is warm (be sure it's dry before you use it).

6. Make the toast. Put a small towel or napkin in the oven-proof dish, put the hot toast in and cover it with the corners of whatever cover you are using.

7. Put the toast on the tray, pour the coffee, and carry the full tray—very carefully—into the bedroom to serve.

Substitutes

Coffee
Try tea.

Orange juice
You can use almost any fruit juice that is appropriate for breakfast, such as apple, grape, grapefruit, tomato, and the like.

Toast
Try an English muffin or other kinds of muffins that can be toasted.

Helpful Hints

Make sure you know what your special person likes for breakfast. Why make waffles for your sister's birthday if she is on a diet?

Most people have coffee for breakfast, but some prefer tea. As a surprise try a new kind of tea. Check the market shelves for different kinds of packaged teas.

If you decide you want to buy a tray cloth or napkins, make sure the material is a drip-dry, or a "poly-cotton blend." Easy to take care of, and pleasant to look at.

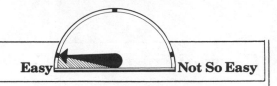
Unusual Frostings for Cakes

Have you ever wanted to put a special frosting on a freshly baked cake? Something different from the usual. These frosting recipes are not as quick as the usual frostings, but they are unusual. Choose carefully to match the cake with the frosting that suits it best. A strawberry cake with minted frosting is for enemies.

Servings: each frosting covers 1 large single-layer cake (or 8 cupcakes).

Equipment

2-quart pot

wooden spoon

1-cup measure

blender

2-quart bowl

spatula

fork

Chocolate Mint

Ingredients

1 package flat chocolate mints (often referred to as after-dinner mints)

Directions

1. Place the chocolate mints close together on the top of the cake while it is still warm from the oven. Leave a 1-inch space around the edge of the cake.

2. Put the cake back in the oven for a minute or two—only long enough to melt the chocolates to cover the surface. Turn off the oven.

3. Cool before serving.

Brittle Chocolate

Ingredients

1 large (about ½ pound) package of your favorite chocolate bar—one made with goodies such as nuts or raisins.

Directions

1. Melt the chocolate over very low heat, stirring all the time with a wooden spoon so the chocolate does not stick to the bottom of the pot.

2. Spoon the melted candy carefully over the center of the cake and let it run by itself (it creeps, actually) to the edges of the cake.

Fruit Mallow

Ingredients

1 large can (or 2 medium cans) of peaches, drained

half of a 16-ounce jar of marshmallow fluff

Directions

1. Put the peaches into the blender. Set at the "crumb/grind" and whirl them a few times.

2. Add one-half jar marshmallow fluff and blend until mixed, but not smooth.

3. Spoon onto cake.

Roasty-Toasty

Ingredients

1 8-ounce can crushed pineapple, drained

1 cup shredded coconut

¾ cup soft brown sugar

¾ stick margarine

Continued

Directions

1. Combine soft brown sugar and margarine in a bowl, using a fork.

2. Add the coconut and the pineapple. Mix well.

3. Spread the mixture on the cake.

4. Put the cake under the broiler until the frosting bubbles (about 4 minutes).

Helpful Hints

If any frosting is too thin, thicken it with powdered sugar or whipped cream.

The liquid part of almost any frosting recipe can usually be substituted with chocolate syrup.

If you want chopped nuts in your frosting, and the recipe has sugar in it, put the nuts and the sugar in a blender and blend them until the nuts are ground. Nuts alone turn very oily and can stop the blender. In most recipes the sugar is in a much larger quantity than the nuts, and putting them in the blender together can prevent this.

Chocolate comes from the cacao pod. It is different from carob, so you cannot make a straight swap of one for the other. Carob has less of a sharp taste, and contains sugars that alter its function in cooking, compared to chocolate. If you want to use carob, use recipes that specifically call for it.

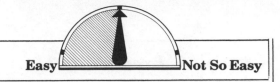
Chocolate Bread

This recipe is a variation of a French chocolate bread. It's rich and delicious.

Servings: 12 slices.

Equipment

rolling pin

cookie sheet (about 15×9×1)

tablespoon

paper towel

teaspoon

spatula

knife with serrated edge

93

Chocolate Bread

Ingredients

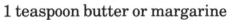

1 package puff pastry

1 teaspoon butter or margarine

2 tablespoons flour

1 8-ounce package of chocolate morsels (semisweet is best)

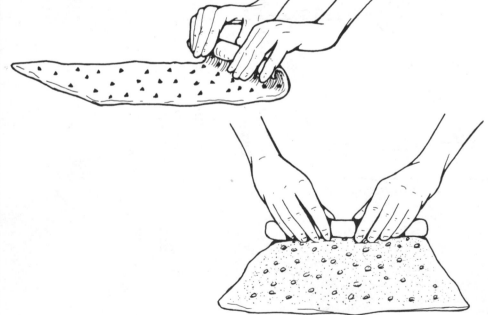

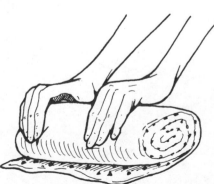

94

Directions

1. Thaw the pastry according to the directions on the package.

2. Preheat oven to 425°F. Be sure there is a shelf in the middle of the oven.

3. Using a piece of paper towel, lightly grease the center of the cookie sheet with the butter or margarine.

4. Roll out the pastry until it is about ⅛ inch thick. Use the flour if it sticks to the counter top or to the rolling pin.

5. Spread the chocolate morsels thinly over the entire sheet of pastry.

6. Take one of the shortest ends of the pastry carefully in your fingers and fold it over about 2 inches.

7. Keep folding the pastry over and over with your fingers until you have a long pastry roll.

8. The open ends should be sticking together by this time, but you may need to pinch them together before you do step 9, moving the roll onto the cookie sheet. It's difficult to avoid spilling the chocolate morsels, so don't worry about it if you lose a few.

9. Lift the pastry roll carefully onto the cookie sheet. You may need a spatula, or even two, to help you place the pastry roll onto the cookie sheet. Or have someone slide the cookie sheet under as you lift the pastry roll carefully a few inches off the counter.

10. Bake for about 40 to 45 minutes. By then the bread should have risen, be medium-golden brown, and flaky. Turn off the oven.

11. Slice when cool, using a serrated knife.

Substitutes

Pastry

Fillo pastry leaves work in this recipe also. You have to have several layers. Fold each layer in threes, and spread the chocolate morsels on top. Place another layer of pastry leaves folded in threes on top of this, spread with chocolate morsels, and continue. If you do more than about four layers, it can get quite difficult to handle when rolling. You need to pinch the ends of this dough, or seal them with water or milk. (Put some water or milk in a saucer and use your fingertips to wet the edges of the dough, then press them together.)

Chocolate

You can't use chocolate syrup or chocolate chips, because they do not give the same results. The pastry gets soggy when it is only supposed to be moist.

Helpful Hints

Rolling the pastry

Your roll will be closer together than this. The picture of the roll is opened so you can see better how to do it.

Cutting into portions

Wait until the pastry cools. Then, using a serrated knife, saw gently back and forth, cutting down at the same time. This way you can get the slices quite thin.

Keeping the bread

It should last for 3 days in a container with a lid.

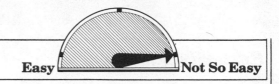
Butterfly Cakes

Sometimes you need a recipe that is quick and can be made (or mostly made) with what you have on hand, and at the same time is special. This is such a recipe. It tastes good; it's different; and it can be a surprise for a relative or friend—or even just something to do on a rainy day.

Servings: 12 cakes.

Equipment

paper towel

12-cup muffin pan

2 medium bowls

sifter

tablespoon

1-cup measure

½-teaspoon measure

teaspoon

rack for cooling

knife with serrated edge

electric hand mixer

97

Ingredients

2 tablespoons oil

about 6 teapoons flour

6 eggs

¾ cup fine or granulated sugar

½ teaspoon baking powder

1 cup cake flour

1 can whipped cream

Directions

1. With a piece of paper towel, oil the insides of the muffin cups thoroughly.

2. Put about ½ teaspoon of flour into each cup. Gently tap the muffin cups against your hand to coat the inside.

3. Preheat the oven to 375°F. Be sure there is a middle shelf in the oven.

4. Crack the eggs carefully and separate them so the whites go in one bowl and the yolks in the other. (If you can't do it using the eggshells, try using a cup. Break the whole egg carefully into the cup, and fish out the yolk with your fingers. You need clean hands and fingernails.) If an egg yolk breaks, keep the whole egg for something else. For this recipe, the egg yolks and whites must be separated.

5. Add the sugar to the bowl containing the egg yolks.

6. Using the electric hand mixer, beat the egg yolks and sugar until they thicken, and turn from yellow to a pale creamy color. Wash the beaters.

7. Sift the flour and baking powder evenly and lightly onto the top of the yolk and sugar mixture.

8. Using the clean hand mixer, whip the egg whites until they are stiff.

9. Using only one beater, fold the sifted flour and baking powder into the yolk and sugar mixture and then add the stiff egg whites and continue folding. The mixture will look a bit lumpy, but that's all right as long as no flour shows.

10. Using a spoon, pour the mixture equally into the muffin cups.

11. Bake for about 25 minutes, or until a golden-brown color and firm to touch. Turn off the oven.

Continued

12. Cool for 10 minutes on a rack, then take cakes out of the muffin cups and let them cool for 30 minutes.

13. With the sharp knife, cut the rounded tops off the cakes, then cut each top in half.

14. Put a large rosette of whipped cream on the flat surface of each cake, and place the two cut rounded tops on top, like wings.

Substitutes

Cake
This golden-colored cake is made without shortening. It is a different kind of cake that has an interesting texture. It tastes slightly eggy.

You can't use most cake mixes because they are processed to give a very open texture, and they'll crumble too much for this recipe. If you want a chocolate butterfly cake, use 3 tablespoons of cocoa in place of 3 tablespoons of cake flour.

Cream
If you want to eat the cakes hot from the oven, you can do so, but the whipped cream will melt and make the cakes a bit gooey (lovely to eat, but a little messy).

The best substitute for the whipped cream is ice cream. One small scoop on top of each cake, push the wings in gently, and sprinkle with your favorite sprinkles. The combination of warm cake and cold ice cream is strange but delicious (somewhat like a famous dessert called Baked Alaska).

Helpful Hints

Many recipes use the word "fold." If you are not taught how to do it by someone, it's tricky to get it exactly right. Often, you will end up "mixing." And "folding" is *not* mixing.

What folding is supposed to do is combine two or more ingredients with beaten egg white (or some other ingredient full of air) without losing the trapped air bubbles. Air expands with heat, and the more air bubbles you have trapped in your batter, the puffier your batter will be.

The following shows you one good way to fold.

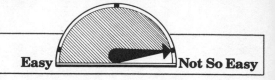
The Cake That Isn't

This cake is called macaroon cake, or macaroon cheese cake. It's an unusual name because it does not have cheese in it, and it is not what we usually think of as cake. What it is, however, is a delicious meringue and pastry mixture. Some people use this for birthday cake when the birthday person can't eat cake or has to avoid egg yolks.

Servings: 4 to 6.

Equipment

rolling pin

2-cup measure

cookie sheet (about 15×9×2)

2-quart bowl

electric hand mixer

paper towel

spatula

Ingredients

1 large square frozen puff pastry

2 tablespoons oil

1 cup fine or granulated sugar

½ cup ground almonds

4 egg whites

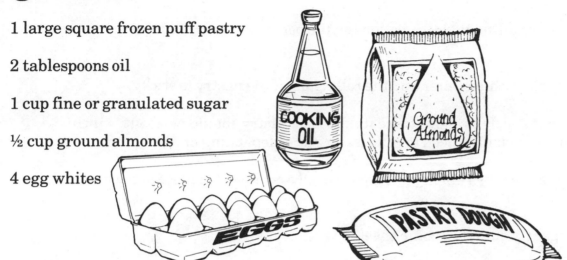

Directions

1. Thaw the pastry according to the directions on the package. Place it on the countertop.

2. You may need to flour the counter and the rolling pin if the pastry is sticky.

3. Roll the pastry out gently to about twice its size. The pastry should be about ⅛ inch thick, which means you may need to roll less, or more, depending on the brand.

4. Grease the cookie sheet by rubbing a teaspoon of oil over it with a piece of paper towel.

5. Lift the pastry gently onto the cookie sheet.

6. Put it in the refrigerator until the topping is ready.

7. Preheat the oven to 350°F. Be sure there is a shelf on the lowest rung of the oven.

8. Put 1 cup of fine or granulated sugar in the 2-cup measure.

9. Put in the ground almonds up to the 1½ cup level. Mix the sugar and almonds well.

10. Separate the eggs. (Save the yolks for another recipe.) Put the egg whites in a bowl. Beat with the electric mixer until stiff.

11. Using just one of the beaters, very gently mix the sugar and almonds into the egg whites.

12. Remove the pastry from the refrigerator and, using the spatula, spread the mixture over the pastry. You can leave a rim of pastry about 1 inch wide, or cover the pastry almost to the edge.

13. Put the cake in the oven and bake for about 30 minutes. It should get golden brown and rise up almost double. Turn off the oven.

14. Then open the oven door and let it continue to dry out for about 40 minutes. (If it's not completely dry, the whites might taste too eggy for some people.)

Substitutes

Pastry
You can use pie crust pastry for this recipe; it works just as well.

Some people do not have much success with the store-bought puff pastry. Here are two substitutes.

1. *Fillo* pastry leaves can be used. Follow the directions on the package. You can also sandwich three pastry leaves together with a very thin layer of your favorite jam and top them with the meringue.
2. Using your favorite plain cookie recipe, roll the pastry out in a sheet or place circles of it in muffin cups. Then cover the sheet or fill the cups with the meringue.

Ground almonds
Substitute any ground nut you like (hazelnuts are delicious). Peanuts whirled to a powder in the blender with some sugar are also good.

Helpful Hints

You don't often need an oven thermometer because many foods—like casseroles or cookies—can survive an oven temperature that is a little uneven. And most household ovens are about 50 degrees different, either up or down, from the temperature they show on the thermostat dial. Puff-type pastries, however, need the exact temperature stated, so it is best to have an oven thermometer when cooking these types of pastries.

Do not do this meringue the day before you intend to serve it because there is so much sugar in it that it develops little "beads" of water on the surface. It's all right to eat (it is only water), but it looks rather odd. The meringue also tastes a little different. Sugar can collect moisture from the air. So does salt, and some other crystalline foods. This is why sugar (and salt) in shakers packs together and gets hard. And it is why sugar and salt are called "hygroscopic."

Here's a neat trick to stop sugar and salt from sticking: Add about 2 tablespoons of rice to the container—according to its size.

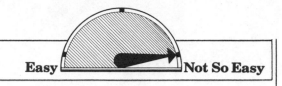

Easy Not So Easy

Father's Day Meal

Here's a special occasion meal for Father's Day. (But remember, you don't need to wait for special days to make special meals.)

Servings: 4 portions.

Equipment

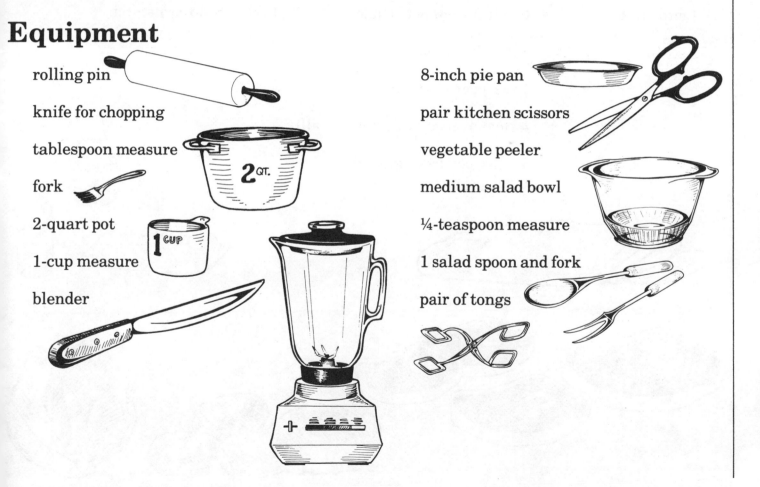

rolling pin

knife for chopping

tablespoon measure

fork

2-quart pot

1-cup measure

blender

8-inch pie pan

pair kitchen scissors

vegetable peeler

medium salad bowl

¼-teaspoon measure

1 salad spoon and fork

pair of tongs

Ingredients

Soup	**Entrée**	**Dessert**
4 medium potatoes	1 medium head lettuce	1 package frozen pastry
1 cup water	4 tablespoons salad oil	4 large apples
1 cup milk	6 tablespoons lemon juice	1 tablespoon cornstarch
2 scallions	1 loaf French bread	2 tablespoons sugar
	1 teaspoon oil (for cooking)	
	4 steaks (about 2½ pounds in all)	
	¼ teaspoon fresh-ground black pepper	

Directions

Dessert

1. Preheat oven to 350°F. Be sure there is a shelf in the middle of the oven.

2. Take a piece of pastry from the package that is about half the size of your 8-inch pie pan.

3. Roll the pastry out until it is a little longer than the pie pan. It does not matter if the edges are a bit ragged—you can always tuck them under. Just don't roll the pastry out to be thinner than about ¼ inch.

4. Cut the apples in quarters and take out the cores. If you are using tart apples, peel them. If you are using crisp eating apples, don't peel them.

5. Slice the apple crosswise and put into the pie pan.

6. Sprinkle the apples with the cornstarch and the sugar.

7. Carefully place the pastry on top of the apples and tuck the edges under.

8. Press the fork around the edge to seal the pastry onto the pie pan.

9. Cut a little hole in the top of the pastry to let the steam escape.

10. Bake the pie in the oven for 35 minutes.

Soup

1. While the pie is baking, scrub the potatoes well, peel, and cut them into small pieces (about the size of a walnut or a little bigger).

2. Put them in the pot with the cup of water and bring to a boil. This should take about 20 minutes (make sure they do not burn).

Continued

3. When the potatoes are soft and there is practically no water left, put them in the blender with the cup of milk.

4. Turn the blender on "puree."

5. After the potatoes and milk are pureed, put the soup mixture in the pot over a very low heat to keep warm. Be sure to turn the blender off.

6. Snip the scallions into small pieces to sprinkle on the soup before you serve it.

Entrée

1. Wash the head of lettuce thoroughly. Dry the leaves and tear into pieces and put them in the salad bowl.

2. Measure the salad oil and lemon juice into a cup and mix well.

3. Cut the French bread into fat chunks (or serve it whole so your guests can cut it for themselves).

4. Now, if the 35 minutes is up, take the pie out of the oven and let it cool.

5. Switch the oven to "broil."

6. After you've greased the steaks with the oil, put them in the broiler. Be sure there is a pan under the steaks to catch the drippings. Turn the steaks with the tongs. How long you broil the steaks depends on how rare, medium, or well-done you want them.

7. Pour salad dressing over the lettuce and then toss it gently. Sprinkle with fresh-ground black pepper.

Serve the soup first (be sure it's warm, but not boiling). Don't forget to sprinkle the scallions on it before you serve it. After the soup, serve the entrée, then the dessert.

Substitutes

Soup

If you think it might be easier, you can do this hot potato soup the day before you intend to serve it. Chill it in the refrigerator, and serve with the fresh scallions snipped on top. It's very good cold. Did you know that the famous French soup called *vichyssoise* is really just cold potato soup? It's extra good if you make it with half milk and half cream.

Entrée

You might want to serve a baked potato with this dish, or a different kind of vegetable. After all, it's no good serving bread, or lettuce salad if your Dad prefers boiled potatoes and green peas. And you should check what kind of salad dressing he likes, too.

Dessert

You could use almost any fruit in the pie. You can choose a fruit like peaches because they keep their shape pretty well. If you choose rhubarb, it shrinks down to almost nothing so you have to really pile the pie plate high. You can use pie crust pastry or the puff pastry. You can even use a package of biscuits, carefully arranging them all over the top of the fruit in the pie plate.

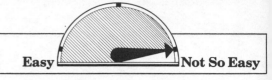

Easy — Not So Easy

French Vanilla Ice Cream Cone Cakes

It is very important to follow the directions for making the cone cakes. The eggs and vanilla in this make it a flavor similar to a rich French vanilla ice cream.

Servings: 12 cone cakes.

Equipment

medium bowl

1-cup measure

sifter

tablespoon

1-teaspoon measure

electric hand mixer

12-cup muffin pan

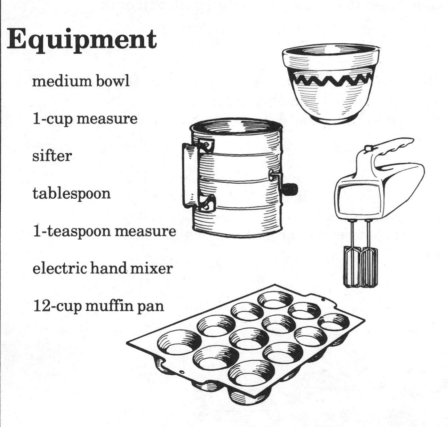

Ingredients

1½ sticks butter or margarine

¾ cup white granulated sugar

3 eggs

1 cup self-rising flour

1 teaspoon vanilla extract

1 package of 12 wafer-style, flat-bottom ice cream cones
(not more than 4 inches high)

decorations: chocolate sprinkles, chocolate syrup, cherries, and the like

French Vanilla Ice Cream Cone Cakes

Directions

1. Preheat the oven to 375°F. Be sure there is a middle shelf in the oven.

2. If you use butter, leave it out to soften at room temperature (about half an hour or more).

3. Put the butter or margarine and sugar in the bowl, and with the electric mixer whip them until they are a pale cream color. (This is known as "creaming," see *Cooking Terms,* page xii.)

4. Add 1 egg to the mixture with 2 teaspoons of flour from the 1 cup of flour.

5. Put the mixer on low and whip thoroughly.

6. If the mixture looks curdled, add 2 more teaspoons of flour and whip on low speed until the flour is mixed in, then on high speed until the curdling disappears (a minute or two only).

7. Whip in the remaining 2 eggs, one at a time, beginning on slow speed.

8. Add the vanilla with the last egg.

9. Sift the remaining flour from the cup gently onto the top of the mixture.

10. With the mixer at its lowest speed, mix the flour in gently but thoroughly.

11. With the spoon and your finger, fill each of the flat-bottom ice cream cones nearly to the top.

12. Put them in the muffin pan. Wipe off any mixture you may have spilled on the cones.

13. Bake them for 25 minutes, until the fillings have risen to a dome shape and are a golden brown color. Turn off the oven.

14. Take out of the oven and let cool for about 20 minutes.

15. Decorate if you wish.

Substitutes

Cone

There is no substitute for the cones. The sugar cones really don't work, even if you carefully carve the points off the bottom. There is too much sugar in the cone, and the shape doesn't work. The only cones that work are those made of wafers that are fairly wide and are flat-bottomed, and not more than 4 inches high. (Of course, you can put the cake in paper cups if you can't find the 4-inch, flat-bottomed cones.)

Cake mix

You can use the cake recipe mix for the butterfly cake (see page 97), but you must add the vanilla to get a more powerful vanilla flavor. Add the vanilla to the recipe after you have creamed the egg and sugar and before you add the flour. You can't use a cake mix, because it will dribble over the edge of the cone. You can add a few chocolate chips to the mix. Or, you can add grated orange rind or lemon ring to get a fruity French vanilla flavor.

Helpful Hints

Margarine is more successful than butter in this recipe because it's easier than waiting for the butter to soften naturally. (If you speed it up by heating the butter, it gets oily and gives you a guaranteed failure.)

If the margarine is a bit hard when it comes straight from the refrigerator, it will take a while to soften. Avoid this by measuring out the margarine first, and cutting it into small bits into the mixing bowl. You can do this by pinching it with your fingers, or cutting it with a butter knife. (You don't need a sharp knife for this because it is too easy for the knife to slide on the oily margarine and you could cut yourself.)

After you have measured all the other ingredients, put the sugar into the bowl with the margarine, put the mixer on low speed, and beat. All the fat and sugar will slowly clump around the beaters and that's what you want. Now is the time to increase the speed of the mixer. The mixture is still rather hard at this stage, and yellow. As the mixer picks up the mixture, everything begins to get softer and creamier. The mixture does not stick to the beaters any longer, and it starts to flow like whipped cream. Keep going until almost all the color has gone: Now that's successful creaming. It should have "fluffed" up a bit in this process, too, because in the whipping you have added air. And this is what dilutes the color.

Nutrition Note

What's the story on fats and illness? It's complicated, and all the answers are not in yet. However, if you are a healthy person of the right weight for your age—don't worry. If you want to make a cake for someone who can't eat butter, find out if that person can eat margarine and then use it in this recipe.

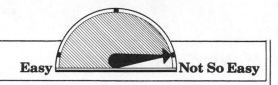
Mother's Day Meal

Mothers deserve a special gift once in a while. And it's nice to give a gift that you know will be appreciated. Well, here is a very easy meal you can do for your mother on her special day that says to her that you appreciate her. (This is also a special gift for Grandmas—after all, they are mothers too.)

Servings: 4 people.

Equipment

1-cup measure

blender

4-quart oven-proof baking dish or casserole

knife for slicing

1-quart pot with lid

large spoon

4 sundae dishes (or similar type dish or glass)

paper towel

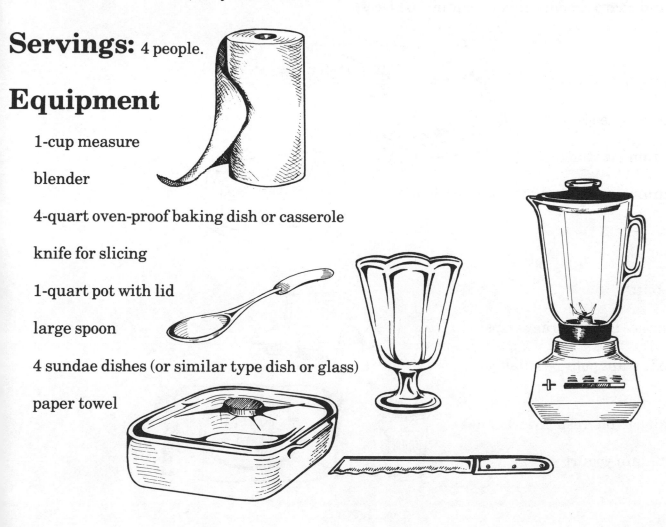

117

Ingredients

Entrée

1½ cups milk

½ pound sharp cheddar cheese (cut into 6 pieces)

4 eggs

12 slices white bread

parmesan cheese

4 medium-size tomatoes

4 medium-size baking potatoes (scrubbed)

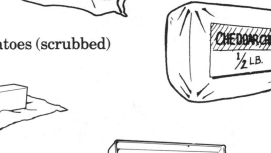

Soup

1 cup milk

1 pat butter

1 16-ounce can asparagus tips

¼ cup instant potatoes (flakes)

Dessert

1 small carton fresh strawberries

1 pint plain yogurt

Directions

Entrée

1. Preheat the oven to 350°F. Be sure there is a middle shelf in the oven.

2. Put the milk, cheese, and eggs in the blender and set on "chop and grind."

3. Blend for about one minute until you see that each piece of cheese is about the size of a dime. (Wash the blender for use in preparing the soup.)

4. Tear the bread into little pieces, also about the size of a dime.

5. Put the bread in the baking dish or casserole.

6. Pour the egg/milk/cheese mixture on top of the bread and stir well.

7. Sprinkle a little parmesan cheese on top.

8. Put the dish in the oven—to one side.

9. Put the scrubbed potatoes in the oven on the shelf (or on a cookie sheet) next to the cheese dish. Bake for 40 or 45 minutes or until the cheese dish is golden-brown color on top. Turn off the oven.

10. Slice the tomatoes and put them in the refrigerator to be served as salad with the cheese and potato entrée.

Soup

While the entrée is cooking, prepare the soup.

1. Put the milk and the pat of butter in the 1-quart pot over a low heat.

Continued

2. Open the can of asparagus and take out four tips and put aside. (Choose nice looking whole ones because they are to float on top of the soup as decoration when the soup is served.)

3. Put the remainder of the asparagus in the clean blender and set at "chop and grind."

4. Mix until all the spears are blended.

5. Put the blended asparagus into the warm milk and continue heating until it is almost boiling. (You can tell by the little bubbles starting to appear around the edges.)

6. Take the soup off the heat, turn the burner off, and stir in the instant potato.

7. Put a lid on the soup to keep it warm until it is served.

Dessert

1. If the strawberries come in a plastic carton with holes in it, run water over the berries to clean them. Otherwise, put them into a colander (a metal bowl with holes in it) and run water over them.

2. Put the berries on a few layers of paper towels to dry. Pick off the green stalks.

3. Check the berries and make sure you remove any dead-looking pink bits (rotten) or whiskers (old).

4. After the berries are dry, put a large spoonful of yogurt into each dessert dish.

5. Then put about three berries on top of the yogurt.

6. Continue making layers of berries and yogurt until the dishes are full.

7. Be sure you end up with a strawberry layer neatly arranged on top.

8. Put in the refrigerator until time to serve.

Serve the soup first (be sure it's warm, but not boiling). Don't forget to float an asparagus tip in each bowl. After the soup, serve the entrée, then the dessert.

Substitutes

Soup
You must use asparagus *tips* because they are completely soft. Other kinds of asparagus—stalks, for instance—can be hard, which is all right for eating, but not for a cream soup. You can use a can of creamed corn instead of asparagus. This is quicker because the creamed corn is already blended. The remainder of the directions will be the same.

Entrée
You can use any kind of good dense white bread, but you can't use any kind of cheese except a sharp cheddar. All the others taste too mild.

If you want crisp skins on the baked potatoes, leave them wet and uncovered while they are baking. If you like the skin to be less crisp, cover them with foil paper before you put them in the oven. (These are steamed potatoes really, not baked.) You can also use yams or sweet potatoes.

Dessert
Blueberries, raspberries, berries of any kind, are good with yogurt. So are other fruits like sliced bananas and peaches. If it is the time of year when fruits are scarce, or you want a fruit that is not in season (say, a melon) check the freezer case at the store. There are lots of packages of frozen fruits that need only to be thawed.

Helpful Hints

Serve the soup before you take the cheese dish out of the oven. If you do this, have the entrée plates ready: put the tomato slices on the plates in a pattern at one side. After you remove the soup bowls, place the entrée plates on the table. Then you can take the cheese entrée straight from the oven to the table so everyone can see how large and fat and puffy and golden brown it is. (Once you cut into it, it sags.)

If you are buying your fresh fruit at the market, always try and peek at the bottom of the little baskets the fruit come in. Berries tend to get squashed and rot at the bottom and you'll never know it if you don't investigate.

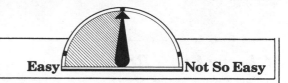

Chewy Fruit Bars

These are lovely when freshly baked. They are heavy and moist and fruity. When a few days old, they are much lighter, and the dates taste stronger. They become dry and more like cookies.

Servings: 27 small bars.

Equipment

knife for chopping

chopping board

baking pan (about 12×9×2)

sifter

1-teaspoon measure

1-cup measure

4-quart bowl

spatula

wooden spoon

wax paper

1 package small paper doilies

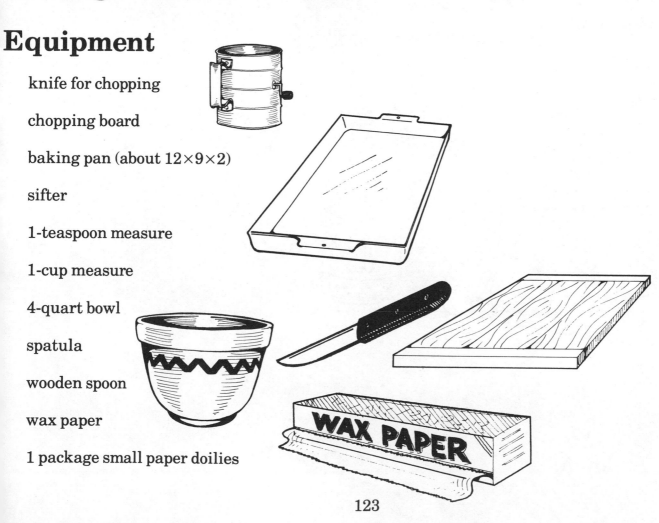

123

Ingredients

1 cup chopped dates

1 cup chopped pecans

1 cup flour

1 cup granulated sugar

1 teaspoon baking powder

3 large eggs

powdered sugar

2 tablespoons cooking oil or margarine

Directions

1. Preheat the oven to 400°F. Be sure there is a middle shelf in the oven.

2. Grease the baking pan with the oil or margarine.

3. Chop the dates into small pieces. If the pecans are in halves, chop them so they are in smaller pieces. (Even a can or package of broken nuts can have whole nuts in it.)

4. Sift the flour, sugar, and baking powder into the large bowl, and add all the dates and nuts. Mix well.

5. Make a well in the center of this mixture and add the eggs.

6. Stir the eggs into the mixture so the yolks and the whites are thoroughly mixed.

7. Using a spatula, scrape all the mixture into the greased baking pan.

8. Place the baking pan in the oven on the middle shelf and bake for 20 minutes. It should be golden-brown and firm to the touch.

9. Remove from the oven and turn the oven off.

10. While the mixture is still hot, cut it into bars. Make eight cuts on the long side, and two cuts on the short side. This gives you a row of three, and a row of nine.

11. Remove the bars carefully from the pan.

12. Sprinkle the powdered sugar on the wax paper, and roll the bars gently in it. Let the bars cool.

13. When the bars are cool, put a layer of them in a container, either a tin or a box with a lid. Place a doily on top, then another layer of bars until the container is full. Seal with tape.

Substitutes

Sugar
You can use brown sugar, but the flavor comes through fairly strong. If you like the flavor, that's fine, but what about your friend who is getting the gift? Consider doing it half white sugar and half brown, which can be very tasty.

Dates and nuts
One 8-ounce package of dates is about 1 cupful if you buy the pitted kind. You can cut up the dates with scissors dipped in flour or sugar. You can substitute apricots or peaches for the dates, but they must be the juicy kind of dried fruit. Some varieties of dried fruits are too *dried*. Nuts of any kind will do.

Helpful Hints

If you really like these chewy fruit bars, there's a way to make them even quicker. Find a supply of airtight containers and measure out all the dry ingredients as directed for one full recipe and put into each container. Then all you have to do is to grease a baking pan, mix in 3 eggs to 1 container of your mixture, and pop it all in the oven per directions. You can keep the containers in the refrigerator until you want to bake.

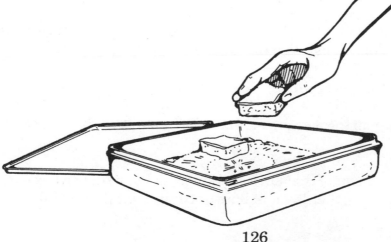

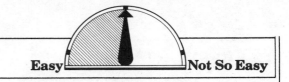

Orange Curd

Curd of this type is often known as "butter." It is not a butter such as the dairy butter we spread on bread. It is more like peanut butter. You can use it as a frosting for a cake, or a filling. It's also good on other foods like toast or crackers.

Servings: about 20 ounces (or enough to fill 10 2-ounce jars).

Equipment

2-ounce jars

grater

sharp knife

double boiler

wooden spoon

Orange Curd

Ingredients

rind and juice of 1 large orange

1 cup sugar

1 stick butter

3 eggs

Directions

1. Rinse out the jars with very hot water. Shake out all excess water, and dry lightly with a clean towel.

2. Use the fine grater to grate the rind of the orange into the top of the double boiler. (Do not grate any of the bitter white pith under the orange skin.)

3. Cut the orange in half and squeeze the juice into the top of the double boiler. Strain the juice for seeds. (If you leave even one, the curd will have a bitter flavor.)

4. Add the sugar, butter, and eggs to the top of the double boiler.

5. Make sure the bottom of the double boiler is filled with hot water. Put it on to boil.

6. Put the top of the double boiler on the bottom and keep stirring the mixture. Once the water boils, lower the heat to keep the water at a steady boil. (Have a kettle of boiling water handy, just in case you need more hot water to add to the bottom of the double boiler.)

7. Stir the orange mixture well with the wooden spoon, making sure it does not stick to the sides of the pot. As it cooks, it will thicken and become a creamy, pale-golden orange color.

8. Pour the hot orange curd into the jars and cover immediately with the jar lids.

9. When curd is cool, store in the refrigerator.

Substitutes

Orange

You can substitute the rind of 2 limes and the juice of 3 limes, or lemons, for the 1 large orange. All the fruits must have good skins, be free of spots, and be of a bright healthy color.

Butter

Margarine in place of the butter simply does not taste the same in this recipe. There is an oily feel to it as well.

Sugar

Brown sugar does not work. It makes the curd taste like bland caramel.

Helpful Hints

To get the most juice out of the fruit, make sure the fruit is clean and dry, then put it on its side and press down firmly with your hand, rolling the fruit across the counter at the same time. This pressing-and-rolling motion breaks up the tissues inside. When you cut the fruit in half and squeeze it, you will get more juice. Do this after you have grated off the peel.

Easy | Not So Easy

Special Dressings

These spicy dressings are very good presents for people who cannot have too much salt, fat, sugar, or calories. Not only are they easy to prepare, but they can help to make meals tastier.

Servings: about 1½ cups for each dressing.

Equipment

2 2-ounce jars

1-tablespoon measure

1-teaspoon measure

½-teaspoon measure

small labels

black pen

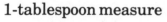
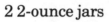

Ingredients

Green Dressing

2 tablespoons green pepper flakes

1 tablespoon onion flakes

1 tablespoon garlic flakes

1 teaspoon dry mustard

½ teaspoon pepper

2 teaspoons celery seed

Red Dressing

1 tablespoon sweet red pepper flakes

1 tablespoon onion flakes

1 teaspoon garlic flakes

½ teaspoon dry mustard

½ teaspoon dry grated lemon peel

1 teaspoon celery seed

Directions

1. Mix all the ingredients of the green dressing together in a small jar with airtight lid.

2. Do the same with the red dressing.

3. Write neatly on a label that you can stick on the jar: "Add 3 tablespoons or more to taste, of this mixture to . . ." Then pick whichever of the following—A, B, or C—is best for the person to whom you are giving the salad mixture.

A.

1 cup oil

½ cup vinegar

B.

¾ cup mayonnaise or salad dressing

¾ cup milk or buttermilk

C.

1 cup tomato juice

½ cup V-8 juice
   (or 1½ cups tomato juice)

Substitutes

You can make the green dressing milder by using parsley instead of green pepper flakes. Or you can zing it up by using hot mustard powder. You can zing up the red dressing by adding ¼ teaspoon of cayenne pepper. (Don't lick your fingers after this one—it will bring tears of regret and pain to your eyes.) Maybe the receiver of this special gift does not like garlic. If you cut the portion down to ½ teaspoon, the dressings will still taste good and spicy.

Jars

If you like these dressings, you can double, or triple, or multiply the recipe as much as you want. Then, of course, you use a larger jar. For small jars, use empty spice jars. Baby food jars are good too.

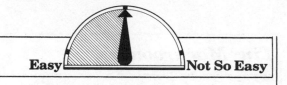

Easy ▮ Not So Easy

Tiny Macaroons

Many macaroons have the taste of almonds because they have almond flavoring added. These macaroons have nothing but real almond nuts in them.

Servings: about 15 little macaroons.

Equipment

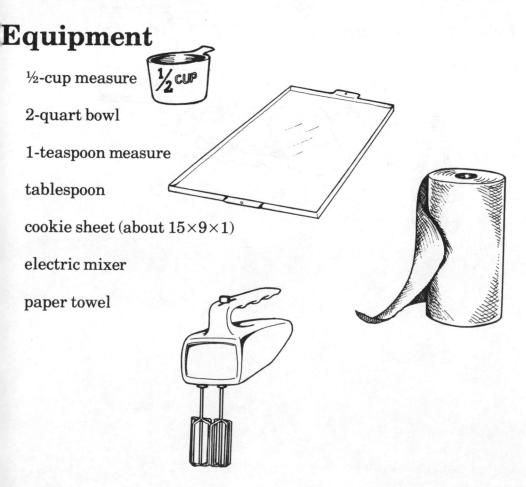

½-cup measure

2-quart bowl

1-teaspoon measure

tablespoon

cookie sheet (about 15×9×1)

electric mixer

paper towel

Ingredients

½ cup sugar (fine, not granulated)

¼ cup ground blanched (no skins), sliced almonds

2 tablespoons, approximately, of ground unblanched (with skins) almonds

1 teaspoon cornstarch (or if you have it, rice flour)

1 egg white from a large or jumbo-size egg

1 teaspoon oil

Directions

1. Preheat the oven to 300°F. Be sure there is a middle shelf in the oven.

2. Mix the sugar, both kinds of almonds, and cornstarch well in the 2-quart bowl.

3. Separate the egg (saving the yolk to use in some other recipe). Using the electric mixer, beat the egg white until it is stiff.

4. Fold the sugar-and-nut combination very carefully into the stiff egg white (for an illustration of how to "fold," see page 101).

5. Grease the cookie sheet with the teaspoon of oil, using the paper towel.

6. Drop a teaspoon of the macaroon mixture onto the cookie sheet. Leave about one inch between each macaroon. (You can put a thin slice of almond on top of each one if you like.)

7. Bake for 20 to 30 minutes. The macaroons should be firm, slightly brown, and crisp when gently touched. They can be eaten warm or cold.

Substitutes

Almonds
You can use almost any kind of nut in this recipe—walnuts, hazelnuts, pecans, and the like. If you use shelled pecans with their skins on and grind them in the blender with sugar to keep them from sticking, the recipe will work, but the macaroons will not puff up as much.

Cornstarch
If you have rice flour available, you are in luck because it will give your macaroons a very special flavor and texture. You can use regular flour, but it will give a slightly different texture to the mix and to the macaroons.

Helpful Hints

These macaroons fit very nicely into the small paper cups usually found in a store-bought box of chocolates. You can put one in each case or two side by side, depending on the size of the case.

If you know you are going to give the macaroons as a gift within a day or two after baking them, you can sandwich two macaroons together with your favorite store-bought butter icing before putting them in the paper cases.

Toffee Squares

These are a kind of candy-cake. They are very rich and sugary, like candy, but the recipe calls for flour, like cake. They have a solid candy topping.

Servings: 28 small squares.

Equipment

teaspoon

sifter

1-cup measure

2-quart bowl

1 electric mixer

baking pan (about 15×9×2)

1-pint pot

paper doilies

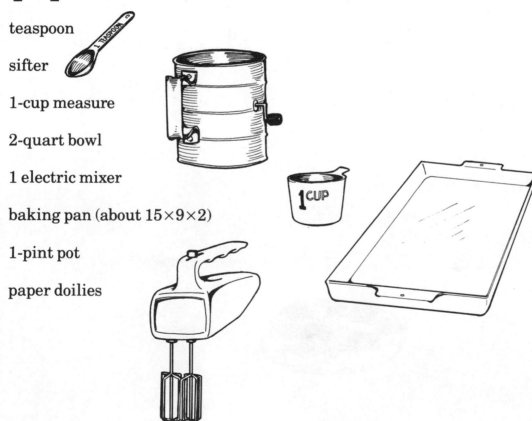

Toffee Squares

Ingredients

2 sticks butter

1 cup soft brown sugar

1 egg

2 cups flour

1 8-ounce raisin-and-nuts chocolate bar

Directions

1. Let the butter get soft at room temperature.

2. Preheat oven to 375°F. Be sure there is a middle shelf in the oven.

3. Put the butter and the brown sugar in the bowl, and with the electric mixer whip them until they are pale in color and puffed up. (This is known as "creaming"—see *Cooking Terms,* page xii.)

4. Add the egg and 1 teaspoon of flour to the bowl and mix at the lowest speed until smooth.

5. Add the remainder of the flour by gently sifting it into the bowl and then mixing it in at the lowest speed. Don't beat the mixture too much or it will stiffen and you will have to flatten it out.

6. Put the toffee dough in the baking pan and into the oven to bake for about 20 minutes or until golden-brown.

7. While the dough is baking, melt the chocolate bar in the small pot over low heat. When the chocolate is melted, turn off the heat.

8. After the toffee dough is baked, take it out of the oven and pour the chocolate over it. Turn off the oven.

9. When the chocolate topping is set—but not hard—and it's cool, cut into 28 small squares.

10. Cool thoroughly and store in an air-tight tin. Place paper doilies between the layers.

Substitutes

If you are going to serve the toffee squares to friends instead of making them a gift, cover them with butter-cream frosting or canned fudge frosting, if it's not too runny.

Candy-cake
You can add chocolate chips or butterscotch chips for a variation if you want. Put them in after you have added and mixed in the flour (between steps 5 and 6 in the directions).

Helpful Hints

Most chocolate bars make a good frosting. The kinds of chocolate bars puffed up with air lose the air when they are heated. And sometimes the nuts will get a bit soft. If you use plain chocolate, add your own goodies such as tiny marshmallows, tiny candies of any kind, little flower sprinkles. White chocolate with chocolate sprinkles on top is really attractive.

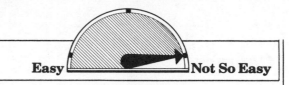
Chutney

Chutney can be a way of preserving many fruits and vegetables. Most chutney recipes have the following ingredients in common: the spices (except the amount of spice you use does change a little), and the vinegars, and the sugars. Apart from that, almost anything goes. Chutneys are a good way to use an overabundance of vegetables from your garden. If you find yourself up to your knees in ripe cucumbers that must be eaten immediately, a chutney recipe can come in handy.

Servings: about 1 quart.

Equipment

4 jars with lids (jam jars about 8 ounces in size will do)

½-cup measure   2-quart pot

1-cup measure   wooden spoon

knife for chopping

chopping board

½-teaspoon measure

1 teaball (A teaball is a small metal container with holes in it in which you can put a teaspoon of tea in order to make a cup of tea. If you don't have one, you can cut a square of gauze—about 4 inches by 4 inches— tie the corners together with a piece of string, put in the pot, and tie one end of the string to the pot handle)

Ingredients

½ cup golden raisins

½ cup dark raisins

1 cup chopped onions

3 cups chopped green tomatoes, or small, chopped and seeded
   cucumbers, or chopped green apples (or a mix of two or more of these)

2 cups white vinegar

1 cup sugar

½ teaspoon each of cinnamon, allspice, ground clove

½ teaball of pickling spice (or ½ teaspoon if you are using a gauze square)

144

Directions

1. Wash out the jars. Rinse them well with very hot water.

2. Put *all* the ingredients together in the pot.

3. Boil for about 1½ hours until the mixture is a pale brown, all mixed together, and with no liquid around the edges of the pot. All the ingredients will have blended together like a loose jam or preserve or relish.

4. Put the mixture, which is now the actual chutney, into the jars, carefully using the wooden spoon. Fill the jars *almost* to the top.

5. Cap them and let them cool.

6. Keep refrigerated.

Substitutes

Vinegar
Any kind of vinegar will do. White vinegar is the cheapest and probably the best if you have never made chutney before. Red vinegar, cider vinegar, and other special vinegars bring their own flavors with them, and they might not go too well with the spices.

Fruit
Mixtures are better than single fruits or vegetables—even mango chutney has other ingredients in it.

Onion is always good for flavor and blending other flavors together.

Raisins, currants, dried apricots or peaches add a lovely fruity-sweet flavor. You can use some fresh fruits (apples are very good) but watch out for watery fruits and vegetables such as *large* cucumbers or *large* squash. (Use young, small cucumber or squash and cut out all the seeds.) Melons that are extra ripe, plums, and whole small onions are particularly watery. It may take longer to boil the chutney if you use these fruits and vegetables. You can help avoid this by adding extra amounts of golden raisins or currants.

Leafy vegetables such as spinach, lettuce, chard and the like are not often used. Broccoli, potatoes, and cauliflower are fine, but are not usually used because the broccoli becomes a strange color and does not look very appetizing. The potatoes can get crunchy and even slimy, which is also not too appetizing. Cauliflower can be good.

Helpful Hints

Chutneys are like relishes and they spark up the food you eat them with so that your appetite increases. Try some chutney on your not-so-favorite vegetable—it just could help.

What do people eat chutney with? Well, historically chutney seems to have come from India. There they served it to spice up the relatively bland rice and vegetables, which were the main parts of the meal. Chutney is good with any cold roast meat, most sandwiches, and is really delicious spread on the bread before you make a grilled cheese sandwich.

Nutrition Notes

Boiling can take much of the "goodness," or vitamins, out of this recipe. You are left, however, with some minerals and some vitamins. Chutney is not a substitute for vegetables—you eat it in such small amounts.

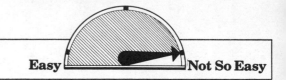
Stained-Glass Cookies

These unusual cookies are very easy to make. They can be a special gift, but they do not keep very well. The candy, which makes the stained glass effect, tends to pick up the moisture in the air, and the cookies can become soft. They should last a few days though.

Servings: about 10 cookies.

Equipment

rolling pin

cookie cutter

small pastry cutter

cookie sheet (about 15×9×1)

wax paper

tea or dish towel

148

Ingredients

1 package cookie dough

2 tablespoons butter or margarine

Hard candy (like Christmas candy) in your favorite colors
(You need about 2 to 3 pieces of candy for each cookie)

Directions

1. Preheat oven to 350°F or according to directions on the package of dough. Be sure there is a middle shelf in the oven.

2. Roll out the cookie dough to about ¼ inch thick.

3. Using the cookie cutter, cut out as many cookies as you can from the dough and put them aside. Put the leftover dough aside also.

4. Use the small pastry cutter to carefully cut a small hole in the center of each of the cookies.

5. Add these small cutouts to the leftover dough.

6. Using a piece of wax paper, lightly butter the cookie sheet.

7. Carefully place the cookies with the holes in them on the cookie sheet.

8. Roll out the leftover dough, and repeat as above until all the dough is used up.

9. Bake the cookies in the oven for about 30 minutes, or the recommended time on the package.

10. While the cookies are baking, crush the candies with the rolling pin. It is easier if you do this with a piece of wax paper over them. A cloth towel (not paper towel) over the wax paper also helps. Do not smash the candies into tiny bits. Break them up into small chunks.

11. When the cookies come out of the oven, place the broken-up hard candy in the holes. You'll need enough candy so when it melts it will fill the hole, but not so much that it covers the cookie.

12. After you have filled the holes, put the cookies back in the oven for a few minutes until the candy is melted.

13. Take the cookies out of the oven and let them cool. Turn off the oven.

14. Peel the cookies carefully off the cookie sheet.

Substitutes

Dough
Almost any cookie dough will work for this recipe, as long as it makes a firm cookie. The cookie is the frame for the candy, so the dough can't be soft or it will soak up the melting candy. And don't add nuts or anything else because the candy might not fill up the hole properly.

Candies
Most hard candy will do. The simple bright colors are the best, like reds, greens, and yellows.

151

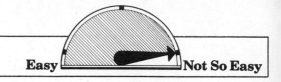
Easy ⟶ Not So Easy

Tangy Candy Balls

This is a soft candy that is a little chewy, pale-brown in color, and tastes a bit as though it has lemon juice in it—it doesn't. It's delicious. Boiled sugar candies need special care, so follow the recipe exactly.

Servings: approximately 3 dozen balls.

Equipment

4-quart pot

wooden spoon

1-cup measure

paper towel

baking pan (about 15×9×2)

knife for slicing

little paper cups

Ingredients

3 cups sugar

1½ cups sour cream

2 tablespoons oil

powdered sugar

Directions

1. Put the sugar and sour cream in the pot and, stirring the mixture, heat over low heat until the sugar melts. Do not stop stirring.

2. After the sugar is melted bring the mixture to a boil over a moderately high heat. You need to stir only occasionally.

3. Turn the heat lower if it boils too fast. (Watch out for this—the mixture can rise up about double in bubbles.)

4. Let it boil for about 15 minutes. By this time it should have started to thicken at the bottom when you occasionally stir it. You can test this by dropping a little of the mixture into cold water. When it's done, it forms a soft ball.

5. Let it cool for about 10 minutes.

6. Beat with wooden spoon until it is thick. It will stop looking glossy and start looking creamy.

7. Grease the baking pan using the paper towel and the oil.

8. Pour the mixture into the greased baking pan and let it cool.

9. When it is cool—but not cold—cut it into small squares.

10. Roll the squares in your hands with powdered sugar, to form the balls.

11. Put them in the little paper cups.

Substitutes

Sour Cream
You can use regular milk instead of sour cream. You then have a plain candy, which isn't as chewy.

Helpful Hints

Add 5 squares of bitter chocolate and ¾ stick of butter to the ingredients and you get tangy chocolate balls or squares. Let the combination stay in the pan to harden.

If the candy gets too hard too quickly, it won't make little balls. You have to watch it, or you'll have tangy squares instead.

Of course, if you do not want to make balls, then put the squares in the little paper cups. Just make sure the squares are small enough to fit.

If the candy boils but does not harden, do not get discouraged. Let it cool, and beat it a little to get it as thick as it will get. Then put it into an empty can. Keep in the refrigerator. You now have an incredibly delicious tangy frosting for a special cake.

Some reasons why candy doesn't always get thick: Not enough beating at the end; not a high enough heat for long enough; stirring too often instead of occasionally.

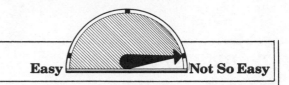

Easy | Not So Easy

Traffic-Light Cookies

These cookies are made from an unusual dough recipe. The dough is rich and eggy and easy to make. It's very crisp when baked. It isn't the usual cookie dough and what you do with it is not usual either. The results are like three cookies in one. They look fantastic and taste delicious.

Servings: about 10 cookies.

Equipment

2-quart bowl

fork

2 cups

rolling pin

small pastry cutter to cut out small circles about the size of a dime or a quarter

large cookie sheet (about 15×9×1)

3 teaspoons

155

Ingredients

⅔ cup cornstarch

1 stick butter

¼ cup sugar (fine, not granulated)

1 egg yolk

½ cup regular flour

2 tablespoons oil

1 small jar each of a green jam (such as gooseberry or greengage),
a red jam (raspberry or strawberry), and a yellow jam (pineapple
or apricot, for instance)

Directions

1. Preheat oven to 350°F. Be sure there is a middle shelf in the oven.

2. Put the butter and the cornstarch into the bowl and rub together with your fingertips until the mixture resembles fine crumbs.

3. Add the sugar to the bowl and mix well.

4. Separate the egg and mix the yolk in with a fork until the mixture binds together. This makes a stiff dough. (Save the egg white for another recipe.)

5. Roll out the dough on a lightly floured board or countertop.

6. Cut the dough in strips that are wide enough and long enough so you can cut three holes about the size of a dime or a quarter in each strip. Leave at least ¼ inch of dough surrounding the holes. All three holes should be about the same size.

7. Place the strips carefully on the lightly greased cookie sheet.

8. Gather up all the leftover dough and squash it together.

9. Roll out this ball and cut it into strips exactly as wide and as long as the strips with the holes in them. Do *not* make holes in these strips of dough. They are the bottoms for the 3-holed strips of dough.

Continued

10. Put these strips on the cookie sheet also. Bake for about 20 minutes, or until they are crisp and the top is firm to the touch.

11. Take out of the oven. Turn the oven off.

12. When the pastry strips are cool enough to handle, take a solid strip of pastry and put a full teaspoon of the red jam at one end of the strip. Use a second teaspoon for the yellow jam in the middle of the strip, and a third teaspoon for the green jam at the other end of the strip. Then take a three-hole pastry strip and sandwich it on the top so the jam rises up through the holes. Always make sure the yellow jam is in the middle hole. Presto: a traffic-light cookie.

Substitutes

Dough
You can use your favorite plain cookie recipe if you have one, but it has to make a fairly firm crispy cookie that can be sandwiched together without breaking.

Jams
You can use any green, yellow or red jams for these cookies. Purple grape jelly does not work. (Whoever heard of a purple traffic light?)

If you do not have the red and green colors, you can use apricot jelly or jam because they can be made green or red with vegetable dyes. Make sure you read the labels carefully to find out if the dyes are edible.

Index

Paperbounds from Consumer Reports Books

Cookbook for Kids by Hilary Brown and the Editors of Consumer Reports Books. 40 child-tested recipes for the beginning cook. 1984. $10

Carpentry for Children by Lester Walker. For kids who like do-it-yourself building projects. 1982. CU edition, $11

The Fantastic Bicycles Book by Steven Lindblom. For kids who like to build things. 1980. CU edition, $5

To order: Send payment, including $2.15 for your entire order for postage/handling (in Canada and elsewhere, $4), together with your name and address to Dept. BPP84, Consumer Reports Books, Box C-719, Brooklyn, N.Y. 11205. Please allow 4 to 6 weeks for shipment. Note: Consumers Union publications may not be used for any commercial purpose.